KS3 Science

Book 1

Ed Walsh

Series Editor

Tim Greenway

Ray Oliver

David Taylor

William Collins' dream of knowledge for all began with the publication of his first book in 1819. A self-educated mill worker, he not only enriched millions of lives, but also founded a flourishing publishing house. Today, staying true to this spirit, Collins books are packed with inspiration, innovation and a practical expertise. They place you at the centre of a world of possibility and give you exactly what you need to explore it.

Collins. Freedom to teach.

Published by Collins
An imprint of HarperCollinsPublishers
77–85 Fulham Palace Road
Hammersmith
London
W6 8JB

Browse the complete Collins catalogue at
www.collinseducation.com

© HarperCollinsPublishers Limited 2008

10

ISBN-13 978-0-00-726420-9

British Library Cataloguing in Publication Data. A Catalogue record for this publication is available from the British Library.

Commissioned by Cassandra Birmingham
Glossary written by Pam Large
Edited by Camilla Behrens, Rachel Hutchings,
Lynn Watkins, and Rosie Parrish
Internal design by Jordan Publishing Design
Page layout and illustrations by eMC Design Ltd, www.emcdesign.org.uk
Illustrations by Stephen Elford, Peters & Zabransky and Laszlo Veres

Production by Arjen Jansen
Printed and bound by Printing Express, Hong Kong

Mixed Sources
Product group from well-managed
forests and other controlled sources
www.fsc.org Cert no. SW-COC-1806
© 1996 Forest Stewardship Council
FSC

FSC is a non-profit international organisation established to promote the responsible management of the world's forests. Products carrying the FSC label are independently certified to assure consumers that they come from forests that are managed to meet the social, economic and ecological needs of present and future generations.

Find out more about HarperCollins and the environment at
www.harpercollins.co.uk/green

Contents

Introduction

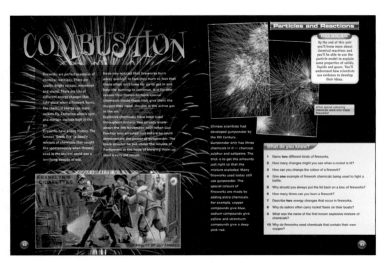

Exciting Topic Openers

Every topic begins with a fascinating and engaging article to introduce the **topic**. You can go through the questions to see how much you already know – and you and your teacher can use your answers to see what level you are at, at the start of the topic. You can also see what the big ideas you will cover in this topic.

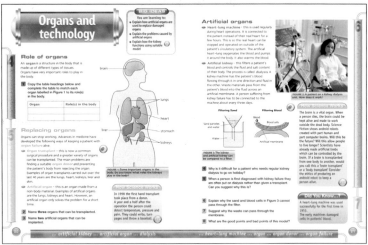

Levelled Lessons

The colour coded levels at the side of the page increase as you progress through the lesson – so you can always see how you are learning new things, gaining new skills and **boosting** your level.

Throughout the book, look out for fascinating facts and for hints on how to avoid making common mistakes.

The keywords along the bottom can be looked up in the glossary at the back of the book. The mouse icons indicate a resource on the Interactive Book CD-ROM.

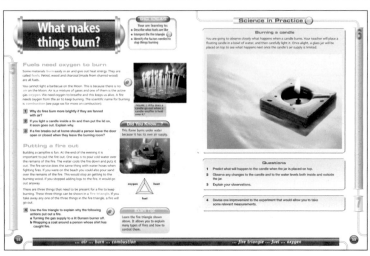

Get Practical

Practicals are what Science is all about! These lessons give you instructions on how to carry out your experiments or investigations, as well as learning about the Science behind it.

Look out for the HSW icons throughout all of the lessons – this is where you are learning about How Science Works.

Welcome to Collins KS3 Science!

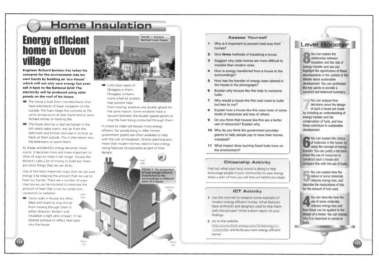

Mid-Topic Assessments

About half way through the Topic you get a chance to see how much you've learned already about the big ideas by answering questions on a stimulating article. The Level Booster allows you to see for yourself what level your answers will reach – and what more you would need to add to your answers to go up to the next level. There are also opportunities here to see how the Topic relates to other Subjects you are studying.

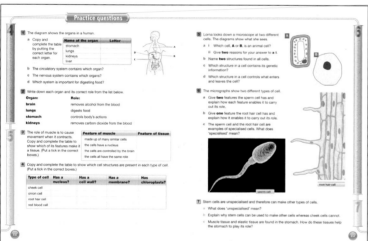

Practice Questions

At the end of the Topic you can use these questions to test what you have learned. The questions are all levelled so you can stretch yourself as far as possible!

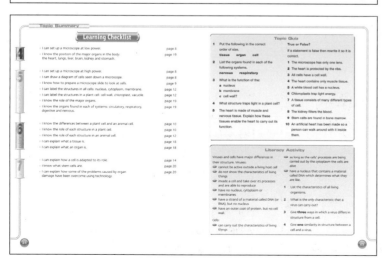

Topic Summary

Tick off what you have learned in the levelled Learning checklist - you can then see at a glance what you might need to go back and revise again. There's a fun Quiz and an activity linked in to another subject so you can be really sure you've got the Topic covered before you move on to the next one.

Microscopes
through the ages

Can you guess what this is a photograph of? It is a single grain of sand all the way from the Sahara desert, shown at ×100 magnification! The image has been captured using a high-powered modern microscope, and it shows how far technology has come since the very first microscopes were developed.

b A very modern vacuum microscope.

a An early microscope.

Microscopes opened up a previously unseen world to scientists. This was a very exciting time for scientists – they used their microscopes to study all forms of small animals, body fluids and water. Then scientists in other areas of science realised that microscopes would be useful to them – chemists studied crystals, technologists checked silicon chips used in computers and engineers looked at faults in metal structures.

Today scientists use microscopes to trace very tiny particles entering the body as part of their research into cures for diseases such as cancer.

BIG IDEAS

By the end of this unit you will know more about the various organs in the body and their functions. You will be able to describe how they are composed of tissues, and how the tissues are composed of cells. You will also be able to explain how and why some cells are alike, and others are different. You will have developed your skills of observing and interpreting what you see.

What do you know?

1. What is a microscope used for?

2. Name **three** jobs where a microscope is used.

3. When were the first microscopes used?

4. Why did scientists only find out more about the blood in the 1670s?

5. Why could viruses not be seen before 1938?

6. What optical structure do all microscopes contain?

7. Which microscope would be used to study the contents of a nucleus?

8. Look at the timeline above for the development of the microscope. How have microscopes changed over this time?

9. Why do schools not have electron microscopes?

10. Briefly explain how improvements in microscopes may have benefited scientists.

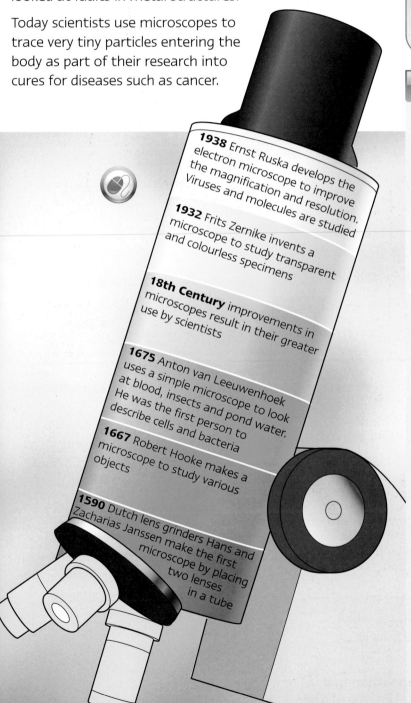

1938 Ernst Ruska develops the electron microscope to improve the magnification and resolution. Viruses and molecules are studied

1932 Frits Zernike invents a microscope to study transparent and colourless specimens

18th Century improvements in microscopes result in their greater use by scientists

1675 Anton van Leeuwenhoek uses a simple microscope to look at blood, insects and pond water. He was the first person to describe cells and bacteria

1667 Robert Hooke makes a microscope to study various objects

1590 Dutch lens grinders Hans and Zacharias Janssen make the first microscope by placing two lenses in a tube

Using a microscope

BIG IDEAS

You are learning to:
- Set up a microscope
- Calculate the magnification for a microscope
- Make observations using a microscope

Setting up a microscope

There are two lenses in a simple **microscope** – the **eyepiece lens** and the **objective lens**.

To set up a microscope in order to look at an object you need to follow these steps.

- Hold the microscope by its base.
- Place it near a light source. (Do not look directly at the Sun.)
- Adjust the mirror until light is reflected up the microscope. (Check this by looking down the microscope.)
- Turn the objective lens to its lowest magnification.

1 What is meant by magnification?

2 Why must you not look at the sun?

3 How many lenses are used to focus on an object?

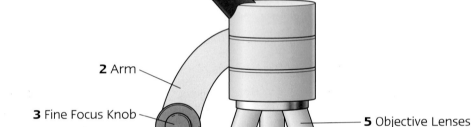

1 Eyepiece

2 Arm

3 Fine Focus Knob

4 Coarse Focus Knob

5 Objective Lenses

6 Stage

9 Aperture

7 Diaphragm

8 Light

9 Base

FIGURE 1: A simple microscope.

Magnification

The **magnification** of a microscope is the product of the objective lens and the eyepiece lens magnifications:

Total magnification = objective magnification × eyepiece lens magnification

4 Work out the magnification for the objects when the eyepiece is ×10 and the objective lens is:
a ×20   **b** ×40.

5 Which lens is changed on a microscope when the magnification is changed?

Exam Tip!

Remember the magnification is worked out by multiplying the lens sizes together, not by adding them.

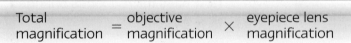

Using hand-lenses and microscopes

Scientists use microscopes to help them develop new materials that combine desirable features. GORE-TEX^R is a material used a lot in clothing for climbers and walkers. It is waterproof and breathable.

You are going to use a hand-lens (or a twisted wire) and a microscope to look at some objects.

Your teacher will provide you with the apparatus that you may need for your observations.

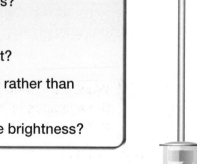

Method:

1 Use a hand-lens to look at the following objects. Write in your notebooks what you see for each one.

- coin
- newspaper print
- scale on a ruler

2 Now use a microscope to study the following objects. Follow steps **3** to **6** carefully. Write in your notebooks what you see for each object.

- coin
- lined paper
- newspaper print
- tissue paper

3 Place a slide on the microscope stage.

4 Looking at the side of the microscope, carefully move the objective lens down (by turning the knobs) so that it is as near to the slide as possible. (Watching from the side as the lens comes down stops you breaking the slide.)

5 Looking down the microscope, slowly turn the focusing knob so the lens moves up and away from the slide. Do this until the specimen is in focus.

6 Keeping the tissue paper slide on the microscope stage, switch to a higher power by carefully turning the objective lens until the higher power lens 'clicks' into position directly above the slide. Slowly turn the focusing knobs to bring the tissue paper into focus at the higher magnification. Write in your notebook what you see.

Questions

1 Roughly how much bigger did the hand-lens appear to make the objects?

2 The hand-lens has a magnification of ×10. Explain what this means.

3 What was strange about the writing in the newspaper that you looked at?

4 What might happen if you wound the lens down towards the glass slide rather than away?

5 When you look at objects under high magnification what happens to the brightness?

6 What problem is caused when you look at an object that is not flat?

Studying plant cells

BIG IDEAS

You are learning to:
- Explain the role of a plant cell
- Describe the difference between plant and animal cells
- Record the structure of different types of plant cells

Building blocks in plants

Plant **cells** are the 'building blocks' found in all plants. Each plant cell has the same features as an animal cell and also contain some other structures too.

Look at the plant cell shown in Figure 2 – it shows the main structures found in all plant cells, for example in the roots and the leaves.

1 Look again at the plant cell in Figure 2. What shape is it?

2 Name **one** type of plant cell.

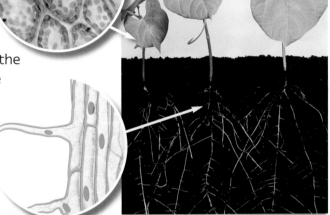

FIGURE 1: Different parts of a plant are made up of the same basic cells but with small differences depending on where they are in the plant.

Studying plant cells

However, not all plant cells are *exactly* the same. For example:

- a **root cell** does not need **chloroplasts** (these absorb sunlight) as its job is to absorb water and minerals from the soil

- to grow a plant needs to 'make' new cells. New plant cells are formed from simple cells found in the growing regions of a plant – the root tip, buds or growth rings. These simple cells are called **stem cells**.

Differences between plant and animal cells

The plant cell has the following structures that are *not* found in animal cells.

- **Cell wall** – an outer protective layer that keeps the cell rigid.
- **Chloroplast** – a structure that contains a green pigment that traps light.
- **Cell vacuole** – a fluid-filled space inside the cell that gives the cell its shape.

3 Which **three** structures are found in both plants and animals?

4 Which **three** structures are only found in plant cells?

5 In a plant cell what is the role of the:
   a cell wall   **b** chloroplast   **c** cell vacuole?

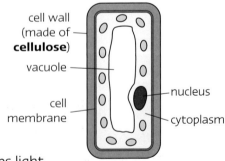

cell wall (made of **cellulose**)

vacuole

cell membrane

nucleus

cytoplasm

FIGURE 2: The different parts of a plant cell.

... cell ... cell vacuole ... cell wall ... cellulose

Be a plant detective!

You are going to prepare and then look at onion cells under the microscope and then draw what you see. You are then going to be a plant detective and match some mystery plant cells to the plants they are taken from. You are then going to make a model of a plant cell. Your teacher will provide you with the apparatus that you need for your investigation.

Method:

1 Collect the plant sample slides labelled 'A' to 'C' and the piece of onion.

2 Take off a piece of onion tissue and carefully peel off the outer layer and place this on a slide. Place a coverslip over the onion sample. Place your slide on the microscope stage.

3 Using the '×10' magnification focus the microscope on the sample.

4 Draw what you see in your notebook. (*Hint:* use the photograph of the onion cells above to help you.) Remember to label your drawing.

5 Now look at each slide in turn labelled 'A' to 'C' under the microscope. Using what you see down the microscope and the photographs on this page match slides 'A' to 'D' with the plant that they are taken from. Write down your answers.

Scientists sometimes make models of what they are looking at to help their understanding. This can be a difficult skill, but it does help them to remember what they find out.

6 You are now going to have a go at building a plant cell model. Hopefully it will help you to remember what a plant cell looks like! Your model can be 2-D or 3-D. Explain to the group what your model shows.

Questions

1 Which structures cannot be seen in the onion cell?

2 Which structure has made the cells green in the leaves of the pond weed?

3 What structures did you see in all the plant cells except for the potato scrapings?

4 How does your model plant cell differ from a model of an animal cell?

5 The growth cells of a plant are small, colourless and consist of cytoplasm and a nucleus. What changes must occur to form a leaf cell?

... *chloroplast ... root cell ... stem cell*

Studying animal cells

BIG IDEAS

You are learning to:
- Describe the structure of an animal cell
- Explain the role of each part of an animal cell
- Construct a model to represent a cell

What are we made of?

A cell is a building block of an **organism**. You are made up of millions and millions of cells. Not all cells are the same.

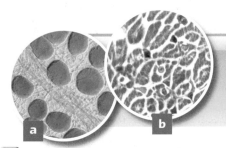

FIGURE 2: **a** Human muscle cells. **b** Human fat cells. What differences are there between the two types of cell?

1 Name **two** types of animal cells.

2 Look again at the animal cell in Figure 1. What shape is it?

Identifying parts of an animal cell

3 Name the structures labelled **A**, **B** and **C** in Figure 3.

Roles of cell structures

Each structure in a cell has a certain **role** (function).

- **Nucleus** – the **control centre**. It gives information on what type of cell is formed.
- **Cell membrane** – an outer delicate layer that contains the contents of the cell and allows substances to enter and leave the cell.
- **Cytoplasm** – jelly-like liquid where cell activity occurs.

4 Copy and complete the table below to show the roles of the main structures in an animal cell.

5 Do you think the nucleus always has to be in the middle of a cell? Give evidence to support your answer.

6 Explain why an animal cell has an irregular shape and a plant cell has a fixed shape.

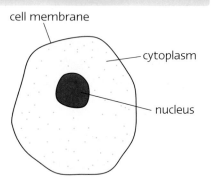

FIGURE 1: A typical animal cell.

cell membrane

cytoplasm

nucleus

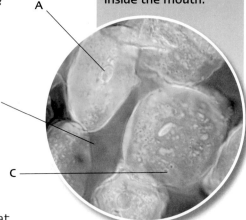

FIGURE 3: Human cheek cells taken from inside the mouth.

A

B

C

Watch Out!

- Cell walls are found only in plant cells.
- Cell membranes are found in both plant and animal cells.

Part of animal cell	Role(s)
nucleus	
cell membrane	
cytoplasm	

... cell membrane ... cytoplasm ... control centre

More about biological drawings

Scientists have to be very skilled at recording what they see so that other people can look at their work. There are different ways of doing this – they can use graphs to show data; they can write reports of investigations; they can make models and they can make detailed biological drawings.

This is an example of a good biological drawing of a white blood cell.

In this practical you are going to prepare a slide of cheek cells and then using your microscope skills you are going to draw some of the cells. You are then going to make a model of an animal cell. Your teacher will provide you with the apparatus that you may need for your study.

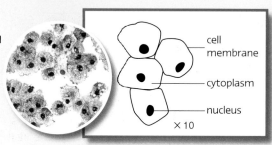

cell membrane

cytoplasm

nucleus

× 10

Method:

1 Prepare your slide of a cheek cell.

2 Place the slide on the microscope stage and focus the microscope on the ×10 magnification.

3 Using a sharp pencil draw what you see. Label your drawing.

4 Look at your partner's drawing to see how well they have done. Ring areas that need improving and tick good points. Use the 'biological drawing checklist' below to award them marks.

5 As you did for the plant cell, you are going to have a go at building an animal cell model. Hopefully it will help you to remember what an animal cell looks like! Your model can be 2-D or 3-D. Explain to the group what your model shows.

Biological drawing checklist

? *Is the drawing labelled clearly and do the label lines point to the correct part of the drawing? If 'yes' give your partner 1 mark.*

? *Is the drawing the same shape as the cell(s) seen down the microscope? If 'yes' give your partner 1 mark.*

? *Is the magnification recorded correctly? If 'yes' give your partner 1 mark.*

? *Has a sharp pencil been used? If 'yes' give your partner 1 mark.*

How did your partner do?

Questions

1 Why is it important to use a sharp pencil in biological drawing?

2 What care must you take when using a slide?

3 Why is a model a useful way of understanding what you see?

4 Why is it difficult to see the cells at high magnification?

5 Surgeons sometimes take samples of cells from a person's body (biopsy). Why might they need to examine the cells?

Designed for a purpose

BIG IDEAS

You are learning to:
- Recognise the cell structure in different cells
- Draw appropriate diagrams of different types of cell
- Explain how the cell structure is related to its function

Different cells suit different roles

Very young cells start out all the same but then they grow and change their shape and structure to become suited to a certain **role**. They become **specialised**.

This applies to many other areas, for example in Technology there are different tools to carry out different jobs. Each tool is suited to a different job – a chisel has a sharp edge at the end for chipping away at a surface, a saw has a serrated edge to help it cut through things.

1 How is a hammer suited to its job?

2 How is a pair of scissors suited to its job?

Specialised cells

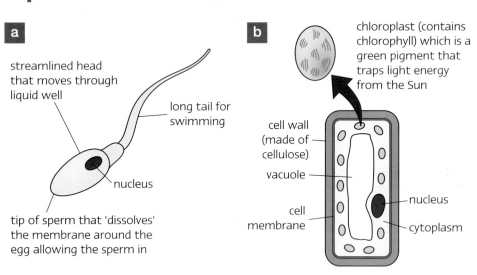

a
- streamlined head that moves through liquid well
- long tail for swimming
- nucleus
- tip of sperm that 'dissolves' the membrane around the egg allowing the sperm in

b
- chloroplast (contains chlorophyll) which is a green pigment that traps light energy from the Sun
- cell wall (made of cellulose)
- vacuole
- cell membrane
- nucleus
- cytoplasm

FIGURE 1: **a** A sperm cell's function is to fertilise an egg. **b** A leaf cell's function is to make sugar (chemical energy). **In what ways are the cells shown here adapted to their functions?**

Each different type of cell has different **key features** that make it suited to the different role(s) that it carries out. The role(s) a cell carries out is called its **function**. For example, a nerve cell is very long and is surrounded by a fatty substance so that it can carry a signal quickly to where it is needed in the body.

3 Give **two** structures in a sperm cell that are found in all cells.

4 Give **two** structures that indicate the leaf cell is a plant cell.

... function ... key feature

When a person breaks their neck or back they can become paralysed because the nerves of the spinal cord are damaged. The nerve cells are not easily repaired. Research scientists have shown they can 'train' cells to grow, one by one, along a chemical trail. Many believe that one day scientists can 'persuade' nerve cells to grow again in order to repair spinal injuries.

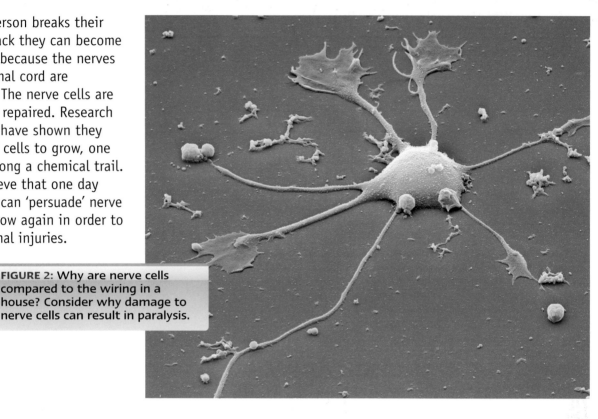

 FIGURE 2: Why are nerve cells compared to the wiring in a house? Consider why damage to nerve cells can result in paralysis.

Why does a cell look like that?

Plants and animals have many other specialised cells.

FIGURE 3: a A root hair cell's function is to take in water from the soil. **b** A red blood cell's function is to carry oxygen.

5 Draw a root hair cell and label its main structures. Explain how it is adapted for taking in water from the soil.

6 Draw a red blood cell and label its main structures. Which structure is missing? How does this allow it to carry more oxygen?

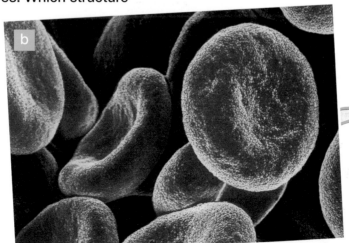

That might sound like science fiction but you can see from the photograph that it is true. Animal tissues have been grown by scientists in laboratories for over 15 years. The process is called bioengineering and involves taking tiny cells and growing them into tissues that can then be used to replace damaged tissues in people.

The first two human tissues that have been grown are the upper layer of the skin and the upper layer of the cornea of the eye.

In order to grow the upper layer of skin the scientists use:

- human stem cells
- an incubator at body temperature
- nutrients for the cells to grow in.

The scientists take a piece of skin, roughly the size of a 10p coin, from a badly burnt patient. The patient's stem cells are isolated from the skin piece. These are grown in a nutrient-rich medium and produce a lot of skin in only a couple of weeks. The skin is important in protecting the body and acting as a sense organ. There are three layers of skin, so third-degree burns means all three layers are damaged.

There has recently been another breakthrough made by Sir Magdi Yacoub, a world famous heart surgeon based in London. He has worked with his team of scientists to grow heart-valve cells by taking stem cells from a patient's bone marrow. The team used a protein of great tensile (pulling) strength to provide a scaffold around which to grow the tissue. The protein held the growing valve in shape as it grew into about 2.5 cm wide disc-shaped valves. Plastic heart valves have been used for a long time to replace faulty

valves in patients. This has caused problems with the patient's body rejecting the new valves (the body recognises them as 'foreign' and mounts an immune response against them). When tissue grown from a patient's stem cells is used there are no problems with rejection.

Assess Yourself

1   Why is a burns victim at risk from infection?

2   Why is it difficult for a burns victim to re-grow skin they have lost?

3   What does 'third-degree burns' mean?

4   What evidence is there that the heart valve is a tissue and your skin is an organ?

5   Explain why stem cells can be used to grow different types of tissues.

6   Why is it difficult to use skin from another person when treating a burns patient?

7   Why do scientists need to grow heart valves in the laboratory?

8   The new heart valves cannot be used in surgery yet. What trials must the scientists carry out? Why must they be carried out?

9   Will scientists one day be able to grow whole organs?

ICT Activity

Use the Internet to find out about the benefits and problems with using 'artificial skin'.

Maths Activity

- Work out the area of skin that covers your body.
- If a person badly burns one leg, what percentage of their skin may be lost?

Level Booster

8 Your answers show advanced understanding of bioengineering, including why scientists must carry out further tests before they can use heart valves.

7 Your answers show an understanding of what problems scientists have in producing organs.

6 Your answers show an understanding of how and why stem cells can be grown into specialised cells. Also an understanding of why the tissues produced cannot be used in other humans.

5 Your answers show an understanding of the difference between cells, tissues and organs.

4 Your answers show an understanding of the function of the skin.

Cells, tissues and organs

BIG IDEAS

You are learning to:
- Explain what a tissue is
- Describe different levels of organisation of cells in an organism
- Explain the importance of the different tissues in an organ

Cell division

Cells **divide** so that an **organism** can grow and also replace its damaged cells.

A cell divides into two new cells. Each new cell is the same as the original cell. Cells of all one type are usually grouped together to form a **tissue**.

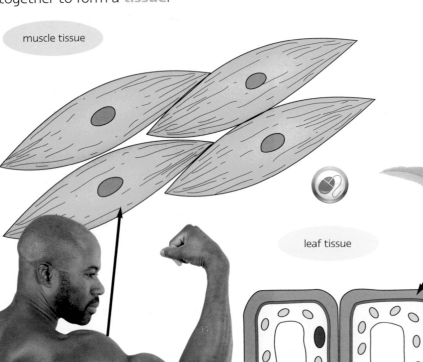

muscle tissue

leaf tissue

How Science Works

Cells can go wrong when they divide. Certain chemicals or ultra-violet light can trigger a cell to become cancerous. **Cancer** is the uncontrolled growth of abnormal cells. The cells form a tumour that does not work like normal tissue and takes nutrients from the body. Why do you think the cancer cells must be removed from the body? What methods are used to remove cancer cells?

FIGURE 1: Two different types of tissue seen under a microscope. What do you notice about the cells in each type of tissue?

1 What features do all muscle cells have?

2 What features do all leaf cells have?

Did You Know...?

The longest nerve cell in your body goes from the big toe to the spinal cord at the base of the back.

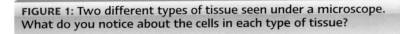
... cancer ... divide ... organ ... organism

Organs

A tissue is made up of a group of similar cells that carry out the same role. Our body is made up of many different types of tissue for example, muscle tissue, bone tissue and nervous tissue.

Sometimes several tissues are grouped together to form structures with set functions. These structures are called **organs**. Our body has many organs. Some examples are:

- heart – pumps blood to the cells
- kidneys – clean the blood and balance water in body
- brain – allows us to control all parts of our body quickly.

3 Name **three** organs shown in Figure 2 that are not listed above.

4 Name **two** organs found in plants.

Systems

The next level of **organisation** within an organism is a **system**. A system is a series of tissues and organs that work together and carry out a set function.

System	Function
circulatory	transports material around the body in the blood
respiratory	takes oxygen into the body
digestive	breaks down and absorbs food
nervous	detects the environment; controls the body
reproductive	produces new individuals
skeletal	allows movement
excretory	removes waste from the body

FIGURE 2: Some organs of the human body. What is an organ?

5 Which organs are found in the following systems:
   a digestive   **b** circulatory   **c** respiratory?

6 Copy the following and place them in increasing order of organisation.

tissue   cell   system   organism   organ

7 Organs are made up of several different types of tissue. Each tissue plays an important role in the organ function. The heart has to pump blood around the body. It must be able to contract when a nerve impulse reaches it.

   a) Suggest **two** types of tissue found in the heart. Give evidence for your answer.
   b) The heart also contains elastic tissue. Suggest why.
   c) Explain why the stomach contains muscle and elastic tissue.

Organs and technology

BIG IDEAS

You are learning to:

- Explain how artificial organs are used to replace damaged organs
- Explain the problems caused by artificial organs
- Explain how the kidney functions using suitable model

Role of organs

An **organ** is a structure in the body that is made up of different types of tissues. Organs have very important roles to play in the body.

1 Copy the table headings below and complete the table to match each organ labelled in Figure 1 to its role(s) in the body.

Organ	Role(s) in the body

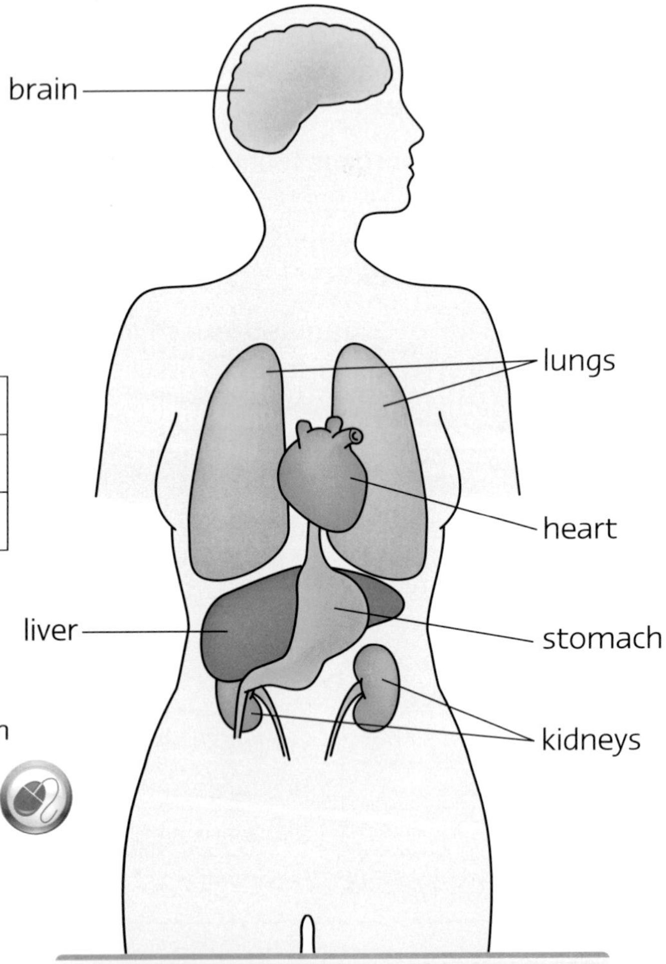

Replacing organs

Organs can stop working. Advances in medicine have developed the following ways of keeping a patient with **organ failure** alive.

- **Organ transplant** – this is now a common surgical procedure and a greater variety of organs can be transplanted. The main problems are finding a suitable **organ donor** and preventing the patient's body from rejecting the organ. Examples of organ transplants carried out over the last 40 years are the lungs, heart, kidneys, liver and skin.

- **Artificial organ** – this is an organ made from a non-body material. Examples of artificial organs are the lungs, kidneys and heart. However, an artificial organ only solves the problem for a short time.

2 Name **three** organs that can be transplanted.

3 Name **two** artificial organs that can be implanted.

FIGURE 1: Some important organs in the body. Do you know what roles the kidneys play in the body?

brain

lungs

heart

liver

stomach

kidneys

How Science works

In 1998 the first hand transplant took place from a donor. A year and a half after the operation the person could detect temperature, pressure and pain. They could write, turn pages and throw a baseball.

... artificial kidney ... artificial organ ... dialysis

Artificial organs

- **Heart-lung machine** – this is used regularly during heart operations. It is connected to the patient instead of their real heart for a few hours. This is so the real heart can be stopped and operated on outside of the patient's circulatory system. The artificial heart-lung oxygenates the blood and pumps it around the body. It also warms the blood.

- **Artificial kidney** – this filters a patient's blood and controls the fluid and salt content of their body. The process is called **dialysis**. A kidney machine has the patient's blood flowing through it in one direction and fluid in the other. Waste materials pass from the patient's blood into the fluid across an artificial membrane. A person suffering from kidney failure has to be connected to the machine about every three days.

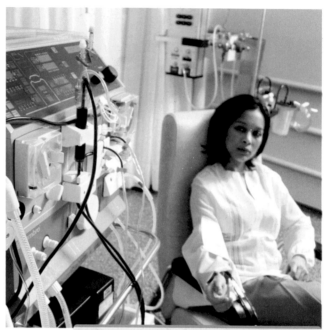

FIGURE 2: A patient on a kidney dialysis unit. How does it work?

Filtering Sand

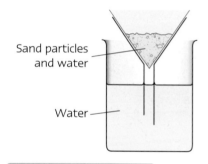

Sand particles and water

Water

Filtering Blood

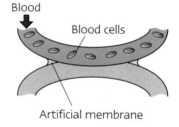

Blood

Blood cells

Artificial membrane

FIGURE 3: The kidney and artificial kidney can be compared to a filter.

4 Why is it difficult for a patient who needs regular kidney dialysis to go on holiday?

5 When a person is first diagnosed with kidney failure they are often put on dialysis rather than given a transplant. Can you suggest why this is?

6 Explain why the sand and blood cells in Figure 3 cannot pass through the filter.

7 Suggest why the waste can pass through the membrane.

8 What are the good points and bad points of this model?

How Science Works

The brain is a vital organ. When a person dies, the brain could be kept alive and made to work outside the dead body. Science Fiction shows android robots created with part human and part computer brains. Will this be the future? Will this allow people to live longer? Scientists have already made artificial limbs which can be controlled by the brain. If a brain is transplanted from one body to another, would you call this a 'brain transplant' or a 'body transplant' Consider the ethics of producing an android robot to keep a person alive.

Did You Know...?

A heart-lung machine was used successfully for the first time in 1953.
The early machines damaged cells in patients' blood.

1 The diagram shows the organs in a human.

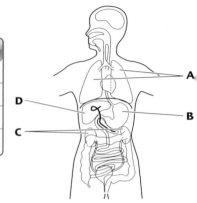

a Copy and complete the table by putting the correct letter for each organ.

Name of the organ	Letter
stomach	
lungs	
kidneys	
liver	

b The circulatory system contains which organ?

c The nervous system contains which organs?

d Which system is important for digesting food?

2 Write down each organ and its correct role from the list below.

Organ:	Role:
brain	removes alcohol from the blood
lungs	digests food
stomach	controls body's actions
kidneys	removes carbon dioxide from the blood

3 The role of muscle is to cause movement when it contracts. Copy and complete the table to show which of its features make it a tissue. (Put a tick in the correct boxes.)

Feature of muscle	Feature of tissue
made up of many similar cells	
the cells have a nucleus	
the cells are controlled by the brain	
the cells all have the same role	

4 Copy and complete the table to show which cell structures are present in each type of cell. (Put a tick in the correct boxes.)

Type of cell	Has a nucleus?	Has a cell wall?	Has a membrane?	Has chloroplasts?
cheek cell				
onion cell				
root hair cell				
red blood cell				

5 Lorna looks down a microscope at two different cells. The diagrams show what she sees.

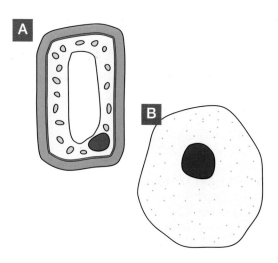

a i Which cell, **A** or **B**, is an animal cell?

   ii Give **two** reasons for your answer to **a i**.

b Name **two** structures found in all cells.

c Which structure in a cell contains its genetic information?

d Which structure in a cell controls what enters and leaves the cell?

6 The micrographs show two different types of cell.

a Give **two** features the sperm cell has and explain how each feature enables it to carry out its role.

b Give **one** feature the root hair cell has and explain how it enables it to carry out its role.

c The sperm cell and the root hair cell are examples of specialised cells. What does 'specialised' mean?

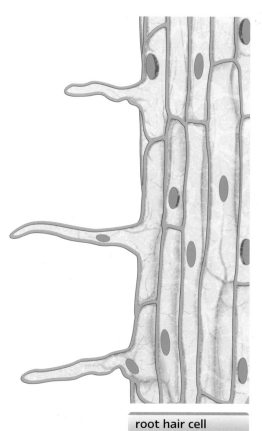

root hair cell

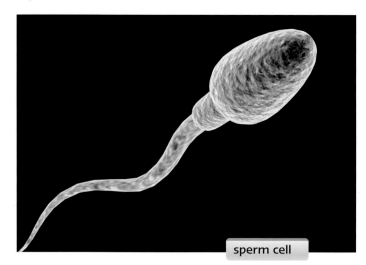

sperm cell

7 Stem cells are unspecialised and therefore can make other types of cells.

a What does 'unspecialised' mean?

b Explain why stem cells can be used to make other cells whereas cheek cells cannot.

c Muscle tissue and elastic tissue are found in the stomach. How do these tissues help the stomach to play its role?

Learning Checklist

4

☆ I can set up a microscope at low power. — page 8

☆ I know the position of the major organs in the body: the heart, lungs, liver, brain, kidney and stomach. — page 19

5

☆ I can set up a microscope at high power. — page 8

☆ I can draw a diagram of cells seen down a microscope. — page 8

☆ I know how to prepare a microscope slide to look at cells. — page 9

☆ I can label the structures in all cells: nucleus, cytoplasm, membrane. — page 12

☆ I can label the structures in a plant cell: cell wall, chloroplast, vacuole. — page 12

☆ I know the role of the major organs. — page 19

☆ I know the organs found in each of systems: circulatory, respiratory, digestive and nervous. — page 19

6

☆ I know the differences between a plant cell and an animal cell. — page 10

☆ I know the role of each structure in a plant cell. — page 10

☆ I know the role of each structure in an animal cell. — page 12

☆ I can explain what a tissue is. — page 18

☆ I can explain what an organ is. — page 18

7

☆ I can explain how a cell is adapted to its role. — page 14

☆ I know what stem cells are. — page 20

☆ I can explain how some of the problems caused by organ damage have been overcome using technology. — page 20

Topic Quiz

1 Put the following in the correct order of size.

tissue   organ   cell

2 List the organs found in each of the following systems.

nervous   respiratory

3 What is the function of the:

a nucleus

b membrane

c cell wall?

4 What structure traps light in a plant cell?

5 The heart is made of muscle and nervous tissue. Explain how these tissues enable the heart to carry out its function.

True or False?

If a statement is false then rewrite it so it is correct.

1 The microscope has only one lens.

2 The heart is protected by the ribs.

3 All cells have a cell wall.

4 The heart contains only muscle tissue.

5 A white blood cell has a nucleus.

6 Chloroplasts trap light energy.

7 A tissue consists of many different types of cell.

8 The kidney filters the blood.

9 Stem cells are found in bone marrow.

10 An artificial heart has been made so a person can walk around with it inside them.

Literacy Activity

Viruses and cells have major differences in their structure. Viruses:

- cannot be active outside a living host cell
- do not show the characteristics of living things
- invade a cell and take over its processes and are able to reproduce
- have no nucleus, cytoplasm or membranes
- have a strand of a material called DNA (or RNA), but no nucleus
- have an outer coat of protein, but no cell wall.

Cells:

- can carry out the characteristics of living things

- as long as the cells' processes are being carried out by the cytoplasm the cells are alive
- have a nucleus that contains a material called DNA which determines what they are like.

1 List the characteristics of all living organisms.

2 What is the only characteristic that a virus can carry out?

3 Give **three** ways in which a virus differs in structure from a cell.

4 Give **one** similarity in structure between a cell and a virus.

Have they got what it takes?

Does your mum or dad ever tell you that being a parent is a tough job? They are not wrong … but as a species, humans have it fairly easy! These male Emperor penguins carry the eggs of their offspring in a pouch above their feet for about 65 days. If they drop the egg – even for a few seconds – the chick may die because of the extreme cold in the Antarctic. That's dedication to the job!

Another example of 'extreme parenting' is the sea turtle. Females lay up to 190 eggs high up on the beach in the hope that even one of these may survive incubation and the journey down the beach and into the sea.

All living organisms reproduce. In animals, the number of offspring produced varies between one to several hundred thousand. All eggs have to be fertilised. Different animals use different methods of fertilisation and development.

- An egg may be fertilised inside the mother who then either:

  – lays the egg protected by an outer shell or tough 'skin'

  – or keeps the egg inside her where it develops.

- Eggs may be fertilised outside of the female by being released into water and mixing with sperm.

When the offspring are produced the mother may give parental care until the babies can survive on their own, but this is not always the case. This can be very important to help the baby survive.

BIG IDEAS

By the end of this unit you will know how the fertilisation of an egg cell by a sperm cell results in an organism. You will be able to explain how a human baby develops. You will have developed your skills of interpreting information in graphs and tables.

What do you know?

1   Name **two** organisms that produce a high number of offspring.

2   Name **two** organisms that produce a low number of offspring.

3   Suggest why fish produce high numbers of offspring.

4   What evidence is there that vertebrates produce high and low numbers of offspring?

5   Do you think mammals produce high or low numbers of offspring?

6   Which of the creatures shown on this page provide parental care?

7   In which of the creatures shown do the offspring develop inside the mother?

8   A scientist is investigating the following question. 'How many baby sea turtles need to survive in order to keep the number of sea turtles constant?' What other information might the scientist need to be able to work this out?

9   **a**   In China the government is trying to limit the number of children in a family to one. Suggest why the government has introduced this measure.

    b   What are the advantages and disadvantages of controlling the number of children born in this way?

    c   How many babies per family need to reach adulthood to maintain the population size in China?

Fertilisation and conception

BIG IDEAS

You are learning to:
- Describe how fertilisation occurs
- Explain what fertilisation means
- Explain the difference between fertilisation and conception

Fertilisation

In order to form a baby a **sperm cell** and an **egg cell** need to come together. They are called the **sex cells**. Eggs come from the female and sperm comes from the male.

When a sperm joins with an egg, the egg is **fertilised**. In different animals fertilisation can happen either inside or outside the female's body.

Watch Out!

The gland that is involved in making sperm in the male is the 'Prostate gland' (**not** the 'Prostrate gland'!).

- **Internal fertilisation** – a male **ejaculates** sperm into a female and the sperm swim inside the female to reach an egg and fertilise it. The male must make sure that the sperm enter the female's reproductive system for internal fertilisation to occur so the male and female reproductive structures must fit together.

Mammals, reptiles and birds fertilise their eggs internally. The eggs then develop inside the mother or are laid, as in the case of birds and reptiles.

- **External fertilisation** – a male releases sperm on to eggs outside the female's body. Fish and amphibians fertilise their eggs externally in water so the eggs and sperm do not dry out.

prostate gland
sperm tube (or vas deferens)
scrotal sac
testis (plural testes)
penis

kidneys
bladder

oviduct (or fallopian tube)
ovary
uterus (or womb)
cervix
vagina

male   female

FIGURE 1: Male and female reproductive structures in the human.

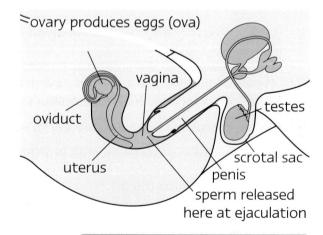

ovary produces eggs (ova)

vagina

oviduct

uterus

testes

scrotal sac
penis
sperm released here at ejaculation

FIGURE 2: Internal fertilisation in humans.

... conception ... egg cell ... ejaculate ... embryo ... fertilise

Mating

In humans and other mammals the male becomes aroused during mating and their penis becomes rigid because more blood is pumped into it. The penis is inserted into the female's vagina (see Figure 2).

The penis is moved back and forth and this stimulates the release of sperm from the testes. Fluid is added to make **semen**. The semen is then ejaculated out of the penis into the female's vagina. This process is called **sexual intercourse**.

The sperm then swim through the female's uterus and into one of the oviducts.

It is in an oviduct that the sperm fertilise an ovum (egg).

Only a small number of sperm survive to reach an ovum and only one sperm cell can fertilise an egg.

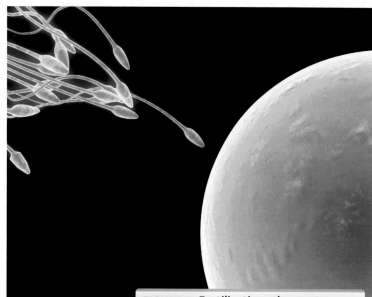

FIGURE 3: Fertilisation; the sperm have swum into an oviduct and have reached an ovum but just one sperm will be successful at penetrating the egg membrane.

Conception

Once an egg is fertilised it divides many times to form an **embryo**. In humans the dividing egg travels down the oviduct to the uterus. In the uterus the egg embeds into the lining. **Conception** occurs when an embryo implants into the lining wall. The uterus wall becomes thickened and rich in blood in preparation for the embryo. If fertilisation does not occur, the unfertilised egg is passed out of the female.

Did You Know...?

- An ectopic pregnancy happens when an embryo implants outside the uterus – usually in the oviduct. These pregnancies are normally unsuccessful.
- Sperm can only survive for about 48 hours once they have been released.
- Eggs can only survive for about 36 hours once they have been released.

1. What are the male sex cells and sex organs of a great white shark called?

2. List the structures the sperm pass through as they travel from the penis to the oviduct.

3. What factors may affect sperm production?

4. What evidence is there that land animals mainly carry out internal fertilisation?

5. Suggest a reason why more eggs are released by fish than by humans.

6. Suggest a reason why the number of sperm produced by fish and humans is fairly similar.

7. Compare and contrast the structures of a sperm and an egg cell.

8. Explain why a couple wanting to have a baby may not be successful straight away.

Courtship

BIG IDEAS

You are learning to:
- Identify the different types of courtship from observations (HSW)
- Explain the purpose of courtship
- Explain the advantage of a dominant male having harems

Attracting a female

Animals carry out **courtship** to **attract** a **mate**. If courtship is successful mating happens and offspring are produced. During courtship the male often marks a **territory** and chooses a nest site, burrow or other suitable place for the female.

In animals the male courts. (This is not always the case in humans.) The male animal may use the following courtship methods.

- Sound – a bird may use song, a lion roars, a cricket rubs its back legs together.
- Scent – males produce chemicals to attract the female.
- Display – males may be brightly coloured or have impressive horns, tusks or antlers.
- Movement – in many cases the male dances around the female to show his ability and well-being.

How many of these ways are used by the human male when he courts a female?

FIGURE 1: A male pigeon carries straw to build a nest for his mate. Why does the male build the nest?

1 a How does the courtship method of a swan differ from that of a peacock?
b How does a male stag attract its mate?
c What problems can be caused if the peacock's plumage is too large?

2 Which animals use song for courtship?

FIGURE 2: Different animals use different methods of courtship.

Aggression in animals

Courtship also enables a male to approach a female without aggression. At times other than the mating season animals prefer to keep their **personal space**. For example, female hamsters are well known for vicious attacks on a male if he approaches at the wrong time.

3 What is meant by someone's 'personal space'?

4 How might an animal show it is getting concerned when you are approaching it?

Smell attracts mates

Chemicals play an important part in attracting a mate and marking a territory. Examples of an animal and an insect that use chemicals in their courtships are:

- male musk deer – marks his territory with musk made in a gland on his nose
- female silk moth – flies at night giving out scent to attract males who fly after her. The strongest male flier mates with her.

5 What might be the advantages of using scent rather than sight to attract a mate?

Harems

Another important purpose of courtship is to enable a female to select the strongest and healthiest mate. In this way her offspring is likely to be strong and healthy. So the better a male's courtship display the more likely it is that the female will choose him to mate with. For example, when a queen bee goes on her mating flight she is chased by male bees (called drones) – it is the fastest flier that reaches her and mates with her.

In certain animals the strongest male passes on his successful features to the offspring of many females. They do this by having **harems**. A harem is where many females, for example in deer, gorillas and walruses, are mated by a single **dominant** male. This causes a problem for the dominant male because he has to defend his harem from other often younger, fitter males who want to take over his females.

6 Why is it important that only the fittest animals breed?

7 What is the benefit to the gorilla species of having harems?

8 Suggest why male birds are often brightly coloured and females are fairly plain.

9 What is the benefit to an animal species of the dominant male breeding with many females?

FIGURE 3: Two male walruses fight aggressively over territory and females. Suggest a purpose for these fights in relation to the success of an animal species.

Becoming an adult

BIG IDEAS

You are learning to:
- Describe the changes occurring at puberty in boys and girls
- Interpret information on the changes occurring in puberty
- Explain the changes occurring in the menstrual cycle

Puberty

Some of the changes of **adolescence** make a male and a female ready to reproduce. The process of reaching sexual maturity is called **puberty**. The table below shows **age ranges** for the start and finish of events in puberty.

Use the information in the table to help you to answer the questions.

Event in puberty	Age range for start of event (years)	Age range for completion of event (years)
height spurt in girls	8.5–14.0	12.5–15.5
development of breasts	8.0–13.0	12.0–18.0
first menstrual period	10.5–15.5	–
height spurt in boys	10.5–16.5	14.0–17.5
growth of penis	10.5–14.5	12.5–16.5
growth of testes	9.5–13.5	14.0–17.0
growth of voice box (larynx)	10.5–14.0	13.0–17.0

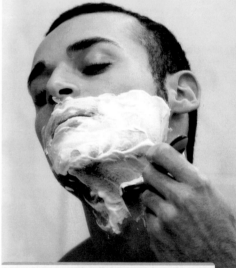

FIGURE 1: Different individuals will experience changes at different ages.

1 What is the youngest age at which a girl starts puberty?

2 What is the oldest age at which a girl finishes puberty?

3 Is it possible for a boy's voice to have broken but for him not to have started his growth spurt? Provide evidence to support your answer.

4 Explain why it is difficult to predict the order of the changes occurring in puberty.

Did You Know...?

This is how the proportions of the body change during growth. A baby has a relatively large head (**A**), but by the time puberty is approached (**C**) the head and body are more in proportion. Diagram **D** shows a typical body at **adolescence** and **E** shows an **adult**.

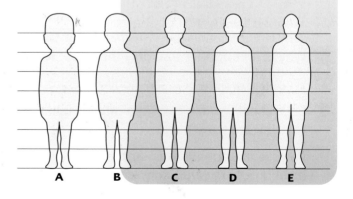

A   B   C   D   E

... adolescence ... adult ... age range ... biological

Menstruation

Menstruation is the time during the **menstrual cycle** when the uterus lining breaks down and is lost through the vagina. A complete menstrual cycle occurs about every 28 days (it varies between girls). The purpose of the menstrual cycle is to prepare the uterus for possible implantation of an embryo. If an egg is not fertilised it is passed out during menstruation.

Beween days 13 to 15 a ripe egg is released.

an egg is produced from the ovary

Between days 15 to 28 the uterus lining builds up ready to receive an embryo.

If no embryo implants, the uterus lining breaks down and is passed out – this is menstruation (or a '**period**') – and lasts about 4 days.

Between days 5 to 13 the uterus lining starts to build up again.

loss of blood

... growth of uterus lining

... uterus lining is thick with blood vessels, ready for implantation

13   15   0   menstruation   5   13

Time (days)

FIGURE 1: The menstrual cycle. What happens during the cycle if an embryo does not implant in the uterus?

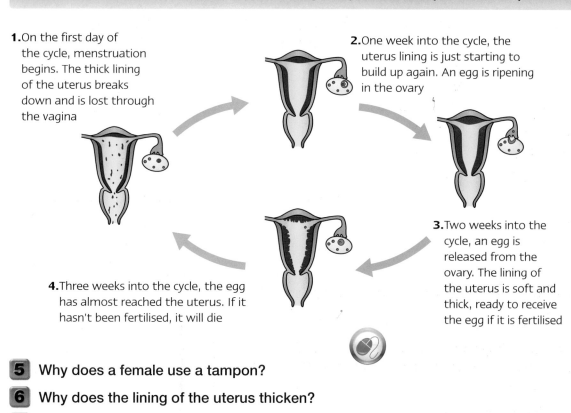

1. On the first day of the cycle, menstruation begins. The thick lining of the uterus breaks down and is lost through the vagina

2. One week into the cycle, the uterus lining is just starting to build up again. An egg is ripening in the ovary

3. Two weeks into the cycle, an egg is released from the ovary. The lining of the uterus is soft and thick, ready to receive the egg if it is fertilised

4. Three weeks into the cycle, the egg has almost reached the uterus. If it hasn't been fertilised, it will die

5 Why does a female use a tampon?

6 Why does the lining of the uterus thicken?

7 Two models are shown of the menstrual cycle. Compare the information. Which model do you think is easier to understand? Explain your answer.

8 Humans have one of the longest periods before they reach sexual maturity. Rabbits can produce offspring after 6 months. Explain the benefits and problems of having offspring so young.

What are twins?

BIG IDEAS

You are learning to:
- Differentiate types of twins
- Explain how different types of twin are formed
- Discuss the problems caused by separating conjoined twins

What are twins?

Twins are formed when babies are born to the same mother at a similar time.

1 Remember that an egg is fertilised and then it develops into a baby. Study the table below and work out which statement **A**, **B** or **C** fits each photograph in Figure 1.

A	The egg is fertilised by the sperm. The egg divides and each of these develops separately to form a baby.
B	Two eggs are released and each is fertilised by a different sperm.
C	The egg is fertilised and divides but instead of completely splitting the parts stay joined.

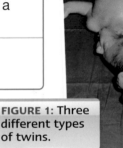

FIGURE 1: Three different types of twins.

2 What types of twins do **A**, **B** and **C** represent? Choose from the list below.

- **Siamese twins (conjoined twins)**
- **identical twins**
- **non-identical twins**

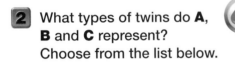

Did You Know...?

The record number of children born to a Russian woman was 69. This was from 27 pregnancies. She produced 16 pairs of twins, seven sets of triplets and four sets of quadruplets!

Did You Know...?

The longest surviving Siamese twins are called Ronnie and Donnie Gaylon, they were born in 1951 and are joined at the sternum. They share many organs.

Can conjoined twins survive?

Some **Siamese** or **conjoined** twins can be easily separated by an operation but others cannot be parted without one or both twins dying.

Case study A – Amy and Angela Lakeburg

The girls were born with a joined heart and liver. Their heart was flawed and the twins would not have survived together into adulthood. Surgery involved sacrificing Amy in order to save Angela, whose chances of survival after surgery were also poor. The hospital where they were delivered advised against separation, but eventually the children's hospital decided that surgery should be attempted. Amy died during the operation and Angela survived for only 10 months after the operation.

3 Do you think surgeons were right to attempt to separate the twins?

Case study B – Hassan and Hussein Abdulrehman

Hassan and Hussein were born in Sudan in 1986. They were joined at the chest and pelvis. The twins were born with three legs between them, but one of the legs was useless. They shared several organs, but it was possible to divide them. Hassan was the weaker twin and the doctors informed his parents that he might not survive the operation. It was felt that if they operated early enough, Hussein would survive.

4 Divide into groups and discuss in your group what decision you would make for the boys' futures. Consider the following points in your discussion:

- the risks involved in an operation
- their quality of life if they stayed joined
- whether one or both boys could be saved.

Remember to give reasons for your decision.

For many women, by the time they reach their late 60s they are looking forward to retirement from work, perhaps helping their sons and daughters in raising their grandchildren. Not so for Adriana Iliescu. Thanks to modern science, at the age of 66 she became the oldest woman to give birth. However, this little girl is not her biological child: the egg and the sperm came from donors.

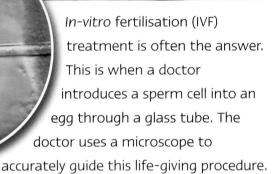

It is far more common than ever before for women to either choose not to have children, or to have their children later in their lives. Reasons for this might include:

- they have dedicated their lives to helping others
- they do not want to lose their independence
- they have never found the right partner
- they put their career first.

As women's fertility often deteriorates after the age of 30, it means that doctors now play an increasingly important role in helping the older woman get pregnant. Fertilisation can only occur when a sperm meets an egg. This means that live sperm have to be in the woman's body when she releases an egg. There is only a short period of time (2 to 3 days) when this can happen. There may also be other reasons why a female or a male is infertile (cannot become pregnant) for example:

- the oviduct may be blocked
- an egg may not be released from the ovary
- the male has a low sperm count (about 2 or 3 million sperm is low; normal is 200 to 300 million).

In-vitro fertilisation (IVF) treatment is often the answer. This is when a doctor introduces a sperm cell into an egg through a glass tube. The doctor uses a microscope to accurately guide this life-giving procedure.

In order to harvest eggs from the woman, she is treated with a chemical called a hormone that makes the eggs start developing in the ovary. The eggs are then removed from her ovary. The sperm are then added to the eggs in a special culture dish ('*in-vitro*' literally means 'in glass') to fertilise them. The eggs are then allowed to divide to form a ball of cells.

The mother is prepared for three fertilised eggs to be placed inside her. There is a 20% chance IVF will be successful. In some cases, two or more of the eggs implant causing multiple births.

If health reasons mean that it would be unsafe or impossible for a woman to have a pregnancy, another woman may agree to have the fertilised eggs implanted into her. She is called a surrogate mother.

Assess Yourself

1 Why might a couple want to have children?

2 Give an example of a career that does not allow a woman to have a child.

3 What does 'infertile' mean?

4 What is **one** cause of infertility in men? Explain why it causes infertility.

5 What are **two** causes of infertility in women? Explain why they cause infertility.

6 Why are three eggs and not one egg replaced inside the mother in IVF?

7 What would be the problems of replacing more than three eggs?

8 What is a surrogate mother? What emotional problems might the surrogate mother experience?

9 Do you think there should be an age limit at which a woman can have IVF treatment? Remember to give a balanced argument and to justify your decision.

10 Compare the similarities and difference between IVF treatment and natural fertilisation.

Citizenship Activity

Write a short piece on what problems you think would be caused when a person cannot have a baby.

Level Booster

8 Your answers demonstrate an extensive knowledge and understanding of IVF treatment through the use of evidence to evaluate the benefits and problems caused in the use of this treatment for women of all ages.

7 Your answers show an advanced understanding of how IVF treatment is carried out and how this differs from natural fertilisation.

6 Your answers show a knowledge and understanding of how fertilisation occurs and the factors that can cause infertility.

5 Your answers show a knowledge of the male and female reproductive organs and cells.

4 Your answers show basic knowledge of how babies are formed.

How a baby develops

BIG IDEAS

You are learning to:
- Describe how a foetus develops in its mother
- Record information on the rate of growth of the foetus
- Explain the role of the placenta

A new life

In **reproduction** a new individual is produced. In mammals the **foetus** develops inside the mother's **uterus** (or womb). The mother provides the embryo with food and oxygen and also protects it. A human baby takes 38 weeks to develop inside its mother. The mother first feels her baby when the foetus starts to move. An **ultrasound scan** carried out in a hospital shows what the baby looks like. A woman begins to show signs of pregnancy at about 6 months, for example her abdomen gets larger and her breasts swell.

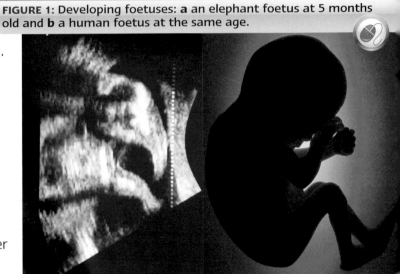

FIGURE 1: Developing foetuses: **a** an elephant foetus at 5 months old and **b** a human foetus at the same age.

How Science Works

Age of embryo (weeks)	Approximate length of embryo (mm)	Developmental features
3	3	The embryo is an oval shape. The central nervous system starts to develop.
5	10	Arms and legs begin to form. The brain and spinal cord take shape. The heart begins to form and beat.
8	25	The embryo is now called a foetus. Fingers and toes appear. Male sex hormone produced in males signals to testes to develop.
12	80	The sex organs start to develop. Breathing movements start. The foetus begins to kick.
16	170	The foetal heart can be heard. The sex of the baby is recognisable.
28	370	The skin is wrinkly. This is the legal age when a baby is viable – even though it could survive at a younger age.
38	460	The baby is ready to be born.

1 Using data from the table draw a line graph on squared paper to show how the length of a foetus changes with time. Label your line to show the main developmental stages of a foetus.

2 A foetus can survive at 25 weeks of age. What approximate length will the foetus be at this time?

... amnion ... antibody ... foetus ... genetic ... placenta

Inside the uterus

Inside its mother the foetus is protected by a bag of fluid called the **amnion**. The foetus is also protected by its mother's thick wall of muscle in the uterus and abdomen.

The doctor can take samples of fluid from the amnion in order to obtain cells from the baby to test for any **genetic** problems. An organ called the **placenta** attaches the baby to the mother's uterus. The **umbilical cord** connects the placenta to the foetus. When a baby is born the cord is cut and tied close to the baby's abdomen – this is the tummy button.

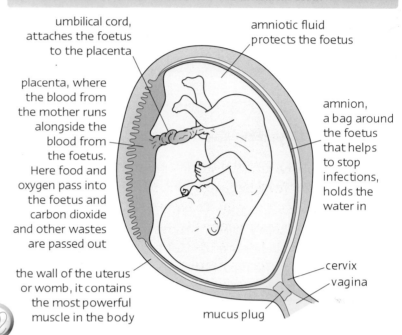

FIGURE 2: The structures that protect and feed the foetus inside the uterus. What is the function of the umbilical cord?

- umbilical cord, attaches the foetus to the placenta
- amniotic fluid protects the foetus
- placenta, where the blood from the mother runs alongside the blood from the foetus. Here food and oxygen pass into the foetus and carbon dioxide and other wastes are passed out
- amnion, a bag around the foetus that helps to stop infections, holds the water in
- the wall of the uterus or womb, it contains the most powerful muscle in the body
- cervix
- vagina
- mucus plug

Feeding the foetus

The placenta is rich in blood vessels from the foetus and mother. Oxygen and food products pass from the mother's blood into the foetus's blood and carbon dioxide and other wastes pass from the foetus's blood to the mother's blood (see Figure 2). **Antibodies** are also given to the foetus by the mother. Unfortunately certain drugs and viruses can pass into the foetus's blood. This can result in the baby being born with a disease or even with a disability.

1. Give **two** features that show a foetus is alive inside its mother.

2. Explain how the foetus is protected inside the mother.

3. Which part of the cells from the foetus are used to study genetic problems?

4. Why is the foetus observed using ultrasound and not x-rays?

5. Explain why it is possible for a baby to be born addicted to heroin.

6. Why is it important that the uterus is made of muscle and elastic tissue?

7. Explain how the placenta acts as the lungs for the foetus.

8. Using your knowledge of organs, explain which other organs the placenta acts as.

Birth of the baby

BIG IDEAS

You are learning to:
- Describe what happens during labour
- Recognise the difference between birth and labour
- Discuss the problems that can occur during birth

The baby is coming!

During **pregnancy** a woman's body prepares for the birth of her baby. A new life will soon be born. The mother is usually pregnant for 38 weeks (about 9 months).

When the baby is ready to be born the mother goes into **labour**. This is when the muscles in her uterus start to **contract**. The mother's waters break. This is when the fluid in the amniotic sac that the baby floats in is passed out. The baby is now ready to be **delivered**.

The baby's head is usually pointing down when delivery begins. It is the widest part of the baby.

1 For how long does a human pregnancy usually last?

2 What could contractions of the uterus mean?

FIGURE 1: A woman near to the end of her pregnancy. It is important that a woman keeps fit whilst she is pregnant.

What is labour?

The uterus muscles contract more often and more powerfully as labour progresses. The action of the muscles pushes the baby towards the **cervix**. The mother may help in this process by pushing down on the baby as she breathes using her stomach muscles.

The baby's head is pushed through the cervix and into the vagina and then out of the mother's body. Most babies weigh between 2 and 4.5 kg (about 6–10 lbs) at **birth**.

Did You Know...?

A baby antelope is able to be up and running within a few hours of its birth.

FIGURE 2: The baby is engaged with its head near to the cervix and is ready to be born once labour has progressed.

Almost at once the baby begins to breathe and the umbilical cord is cut. A few minutes later the **afterbirth** (placenta and cord) is passed out.

3 Suggest why a baby is usually born head first.

4 What is the 'afterbirth'?

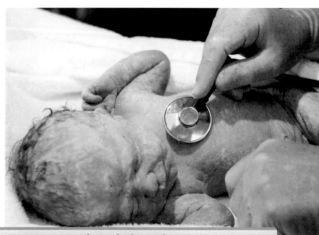

FIGURE 3: A newborn baby. Why must a newborn baby's head always be supported when it is carried?

... afterbirth ... birth ... bond ... breech ... caesarean ... cervix ... contract

Bonding between mother and baby

When a baby is born it is placed on the mother's stomach or breasts. This is important as a **bond** between mother and child needs to form very soon after birth.

A **midwife** then carries out medical checks on the newborn baby to make sure it is healthy. The mother starts to produce milk for the baby straightaway and the action of the baby feeding stimulates the mother's breasts to make more milk.

5 Suggest what types of checks a midwife may carry out.

6 Why is it important that there is early contact between the parents and their baby?

FIGURE 4: A mother bonding with the newborn baby. Suggest why bonding is important.

Complications

Instead of being born head-first, some babies turn around inside their mother so that their bottom comes out first. Thus is called a **breech** position and a doctor often tries to turn the baby around in the mother by pushing or massaging the mother's abdomen, so the baby turns round and is born head-first.

In some cases the doctor may decide the baby must be removed through the mother's stomach in a **caesarean** birth.

The baby may be born early (**premature**). In this case the baby is put in an **incubator** for the first few days or weeks of its life.

7 Prepare a scientific poster for your class to explain what a caesarean birth is and why it may have to occur.

8 Explain why premature babies are placed in an incubator.

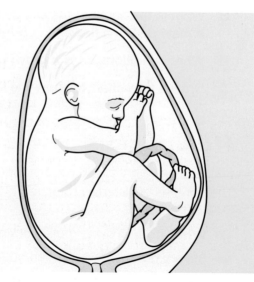

Reproduction in flowering plants

BIG IDEAS

You are learning to:
- Describe the male and female reproductive organs and cells of plants
- Explain the differences between pollination and fertilisation
- From observation describe the difference between insect and wind-pollinated flowers

Flowers

A plant's **sex organs** are found in its **flower**.

A flower is adapted to attract insects by having:

- brightly coloured petals
- a strong scent
- nectar.

Insects are most common in late spring and summer.

1 What attracts insects to a flower?

2 Why do few plants flower in early spring?

A **pollen** grain is brought from another flower by the wind or on an insect's hairs. This is called **pollination**

↓

The pollen grain is trapped on the sticky surface of the **stigma**

↓

It then 'grows' down through the stigma and **style** and through the **ovary** wall to reach the **egg**

↓

The pollen grain nucleus and the egg nucleus join during **fertilisation** and an embryo is formed. This develops into the **seed**

FIGURE 1A: The main steps in pollination and fertilisation in flowering plants.

The male sex organ is called the **stamen** and it produces pollen

The female sex organ is called the ovary and it produces eggs (or ova)

petal

stigma

style

nectary

ovary

egg cell

nucleus

anther ⎫
filament ⎬ stamen, produces pollen grains shown in micrograph below

pollen grain on surface of stigma

pollen grain tube with pollen grain nucleus 'grows' down style to reach the egg cell nucleus

Pollination and fertilisation

The seeds are dispersed so they can start to grow into plants. A seed _germinates_ in the right conditions. For example, the right amounts of water and warmth are important.

3 What is the name of the sex cells in the:
a male part of a flower **b** female part of a flower?

4 What conditions does a growing plant need after it has germinated?

5 Draw a flow chart to show the life-cycle of a flowering plant.

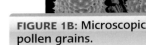

FIGURE 1B: Microscopic pollen grains.

Pollination

Plants have to produce large amounts of pollen (male sex cell) to ensure some grains reach the eggs. The pollen is transferred to other flowers (this is called cross-pollination) by two main methods: insect and wind.

- **Wind pollination** – pollen grains are carried by the wind.
- **Insect pollination** – pollen grains are carried on the hairs of visiting insects.

6 What is the name of the process in which the pollen grain joins to an egg?

7 Why does a plant produce so many seeds?

... egg ... fertilisation ... flower ... germinate ... ovary ... pollen

Why do some flowers not have petals?

Wind-pollinated wheat plants and insect-pollinated apple trees in an orchard.

- Cereal plants such as wheat, barley and oats are very important food crops. They are all wind pollinated.

- Most of the fruit and vegetables that we eat come from plants whose flowers are insect pollinated.

You are going to compare the male and female parts of wind- and insect-pollinated flowers.

Your teacher will provide you with the flowers and any apparatus that you may need for your investigation.

Method:

1 In your notebook draw a table using the headings below and fill in the name of each of your flowers.

Flower part

Wind-pollinated flower. My flower is a _____

Insect-pollinated flower. My flower is a _____

2 Look carefully at the male parts of each of your flowers. Use the hand-lens if necessary. You will need to look at the pollen and the stamen. Record what you observe in your table. (*Hint:* think about the relative sizes and weights of the pollen grains; and the relative lengths of the anthers and their positions in the flower.)

3 Look carefully at the female parts of each of your flowers. Use the hand-lens if necessary. You will need to look at the stigma and the style. Record what you observe in your table. (*Hint:* think about where in the flower the stigmas are; think about the relative lengths of the styles.)

4 Identify the key differences between insect- and wind-pollinated flowers.

5 Write a short report for a scientific article explaining why structural differences in the male and female parts occur in wind-pollinated and insect-pollinated flowers. Mention in your report how flowers are adapted to their function.

Questions

1 Why do wind-pollinated plants produce a lot of pollen?

2 Why must pollen be lightweight?

3 Explain why flowers that rely on wind pollination do not have brightly coloured petals or nectaries.

4 Why does a flower die once the eggs in its ovary have been fertilised?

1 Most lambs are born in spring.

   a Give **one** advantage to the lambs of being born in spring.

   b Which **two** features from the list below indicate a lamb is a mammal?

      A Is suckled by the mother.   **B** Is born in the spring.

      C Develops inside the mother.   **D** Is laid in an egg.

2 Write down each part of the reproductive system and its correct role from the list below.

Part of the reproductive system:	Role:
testis	produces eggs
ovary	produces sperm

3 **a** Which of the following cells are sex cells?

      A egg   **B** testis

      C ovary   **D** sperm

   b Name the structures **A**, **B** and **C** on the diagram.

   c Name **two** ways a foetus is protected in the mother.

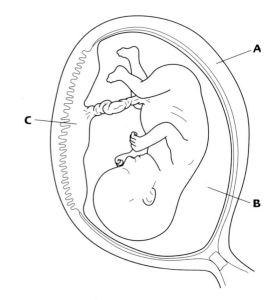

4 The graph below shows change in weight as a child grows into an adult.

   a Between what ages do females grow most rapidly?

   b Between what ages do males grow most rapidly?

   c Explain why growth is most rapid in males and females at these ages.

   d Why does body mass start to level out at age 18 in females and males?

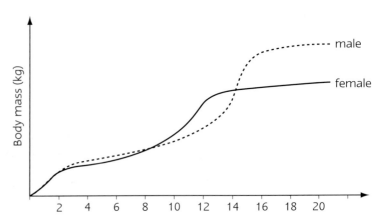

5 A stag (male deer) attracts a female deer in order to mate with her.

a Give **one** method the stag uses to attract the female.

b What is the male sex cell for a stag?

c What is the male sex organ for a stag?

d Explain why the stag produces over 200 million sperm.

6 The following changes occur to teenagers in puberty.

- A growth spurt occurs.
- Periods start.
- Hair grows in the pubic area.
- The voice breaks.
- The hips widen.

a Which changes occur only in males?

b Which changes occur in both males and females?

c Why must the female's hips widen?

d What physical feature shows in an individual after the voice has broken?

7 The diagram shows a sperm cell of a ram.

a Give **one** way a sperm cell is adapted for moving towards the egg.

b Where in the ewe (female sheep) does fertilisation occur?

c Explain how non-identical twin lambs could be formed.

8 The placenta is an important organ in the pregnant mother. It is involved in the exchange of materials between the mother and her baby.

a Name **two** materials that pass from the mother's blood into the baby's blood.

b Name **one** material that passes from the baby's blood into the mother's blood.

c Why is it important that the baby's blood and mother's blood are close together?

d Suggest why a baby shows breathing movements in the uterus?

9 *In-vitro* fertilisation (IVF) treatment is given to a female who has difficulty becoming pregnant. It involves taking sperm from the male and eggs from the female and allowing fertilisation to occur in controlled conditions.

a Why are eggs allowed to divide several times before they are implanted in the female?

b What are the advantages and problems of implanting the fertilised eggs into the females?

c Explain in detail whether two implanted eggs would form identical or non-identical twins.

Learning Checklist

☆ I Know why many eggs are produced in some species.	page 28
☆ I know two ways a male attracts females.	page 30
☆ I know how long pregnancy usually lasts in humans.	page 38
☆ I know the stages of the human life-cycle.	page 38
☆ I know the stages of the plant life-cycle.	page 42
☆ I know that the male sex cell is the sperm and it is produced in the testis.	page 28
☆ I know that the female sex cell is the egg and it is produced in the ovary.	page 28
☆ I know that fertilisation is when an egg joins to a sperm.	page 28
☆ I know that fertilisation usually occurs in the oviduct.	page 28
☆ I can label the male reproductive parts: testis, penis, glands, sperm tube.	page 28
☆ I can label the female reproductive parts: ovary, oviduct, vagina, uterus, cervix	page 28
☆ I know the changes that occur in a male during puberty: voice breaks, hair grows on face and around genitals and in armpits, production of sperm, broadening of shoulders.	page 32
☆ I know the changes that occur in a female during puberty: menstrual cycle starts, hips widen, breasts develop, hair grows in pubic area and in armpits.	page 32
☆ I know that in both males and females there is a growth spurt during puberty.	page 32
☆ I can interpret data about human growth.	page 32
☆ I know how identical and non-identical twins are formed.	page 34
☆ I know the role of the umbilical cord and amniotic fluid during pregnancy.	page 38
☆ I can explain how a sperm is adapted for its role.	page 28
☆ I can explain how IVF treatment is carried out.	page 36
☆ I can explain the role of the placenta in the exchange of oxygen and food from the mother's blood to the baby's blood and carbon dioxide and other wastes from the baby's blood to the mother's blood.	page 38

Topic Quiz

1 Put the following stages of the human life cycle in the correct order.

adult   **teenager**   **foetus**   **child**

2 What is the name of the male sex cell in a rabbit?

3 What is the name of the female sex cell in a blue whale?

4 Give **two** changes that occur in a male in puberty.

5 Give **one** change that occurs in males and females in puberty.

6 Name the process that occurs when a sperm joins with an egg.

7 How are identical twins formed?

8 Does a chicken carry out external fertilisation or internal fertilisation? Describe the process.

9 Explain why the placenta is like a lung for the foetus.

10 Explain why the placenta is like an intestine for the foetus.

True or False?

If a statement is false then rewrite it so it is correct.

1 Eggs are produced by the uterus.

2 The sperm is smaller than the egg.

3 An egg cell is fertilised by a sperm cell.

4 The egg cell is fertilised in the uterus.

5 The fertilised egg is called a foetus up to 8 weeks of development and then it is called an embryo until birth.

6 In all boys puberty starts with the breaking of the voice.

7 The menstrual cycle lasts about 28 days.

8 The foetus is attached to the uterus by the placenta.

9 Identical twins are formed when two eggs are fertilised.

10 Oxygen moves from the mother's blood to the foetus's blood in the umbilical cord.

Numeracy Activity

The table right shows the number and size of eggs for different animals.

1 Which animals in the table are:

   a mammals   **c** fish   **e** reptiles ?
   b birds   **d** amphibians

2 Which is the largest animal?

3 Which is the smallest animal?

4 Humans have a pregnancy length of about 38 weeks. Why do carp fish not become pregnant?

5 For each of the following indicate the relationships, if any. Give the evidence from the table for your decision.

   a Size of animal and number of eggs.
   b Size of animal and size of eggs.
   c Size of egg and number of eggs laid.
   d Number of eggs laid and whether the animal carries out external fertilisation or internal fertilisation.

Animal	Average number female of eggs produced per birth	Size of eggs (mm)
human	1	0.1
blue whale	1	0.1
mouse	6	0.1
chicken	5	30
cod fish	4–6 million	0.15
frog	500–800	1
turtle	120	15

Be smart, be safe!

In Spring 2008 the first ever list of motorbike helmet safety is planned. Motorcyclists will know exactly how safe their helmet is in the event of an accident. The road safety minister said, 'We believe we can save 50 bikers' lives every year if they were to wear helmets of a higher safety standard'.

Many sports encourage athletes to wear head protection. Racing cyclists, horse riders, cricketers, rock climbers and the crews in white-water rafting all need to do this.

Some kinds of head protection are for a completely different reason. Bakers and people who work in food factories wear hairnets to stop hairs falling into the food.

Noise can damage a person's health permanently. Many rock musicians have lost some of their hearing because of the loud music. Using a road drill is very noisy indeed. Ear protectors can save a person's hearing and stop them from becoming deaf.

Imagine you are visiting a factory for the day. What would you need to do if you saw this sign?

A person's eyes are also very easily damaged. Safety glasses are worn by people in lots of jobs. Welders can be hurt by sparks and people who work with unpleasant chemicals want to protect their eyes from splashes.

Special clothing is needed in many jobs. This can be just a laboratory coat or overalls or it can be an aluminium-covered suit as used by fire-fighters. The metal coating reflects the heat given off by the

BIG IDEAS

By the end of this unit you will know why it is important to work safely in science and how to manage hazards such as fire. You'll know what acids and alkalis are, and you'll be able to use the pH scale to indicate this strength. You'll be able to use various pieces of equipment to investigate ideas.

What do you know?

1 State **three** jobs that require workers to wear hard hats.

2 Why is protective clothing worn at some factories?

3 Name **three** sports that require protective clothing to be worn.

4 Give **one** example of head protection that is worn to protect other people.

5 What kind of protective clothing does a house-painter need?

6 Coal miners use special hard hats with a lamp. Explain why.

7 Does cooking a meal at home need protective clothing? Explain your answer.

8 Why do nurses and doctors often wear gloves?

9 Can you think of an example where wearing protective clothing might cause an accident?

10 Do you think all children should be made to wear bicycle helmets when they ride their bikes? Give reasons for your answer.

Safety in the laboratory

BIG IDEAS

You are learning to:
- Recognise hazards in a laboratory
- Decide which hazards are most dangerous
- Explain the importance of clear instructions

Hazards in the laboratory

Once you have worked in a science laboratory, you will understand the **hazards**. Ignoring the hazards can lead to accidents and people being injured. We can easily spot most of the hazards in the lab. They can involve using water, chemicals, heating or other things. Sometimes we cause hazards by the way we behave. Loose clothing can be a hazard if it falls into a flame.

1 Give **two** examples of how water could be dangerous in the laboratory.

2 Give **two** examples of the ways clothing could be dangerous in the laboratory.

FIGURE 1: How many hazards can you spot?

Some of the hazards shown in Figure 1 are connected with apparatus being used incorrectly and others with the way in which students are working.

- Eye protection is essential to protect your eyes. When glass containers break, you can be injured by the glass fragments and by the chemicals inside.

- Using the gas flame of a Bunsen burner has the risk of burning yourself.

... hazard

Use the picture on the right to answer these questions.

3 Which bottle do you think has the worst label in safety terms?

4 Develop a short list of 'Golden Rules' for use in a school laboratory.

5 Design a screen saver based on the theme of laboratory safety.

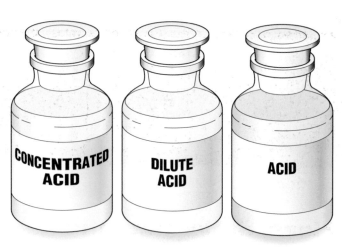

CONCENTRATED ACID

DILUTE ACID

ACID

Listen!

Things can go wrong if students do not listen to instructions. They may mix two chemicals in the wrong order or set up apparatus in an unsafe way so that it falls apart. If students don't give their full attention to their practical work, accidents may happen.

Using safety information

To make copper sulphate solution you first need to stir some of the powder with water in a beaker. The powder can be as fine as dust and is easy to spill. If you stir too fast, the solution may spill out.

6 What safety precautions would be best to prepare this solution safely.

7 What would you do if you spilt some of the solution on your hand?

8 Safety statistics show that most school accidents occur in corridors or playgrounds. Suggest reasons for this. Are schools dangerous places? Justify your answers.

How Science Works

Before starting an investigation, scientists carry out a **risk assessment**. They consider all the possible dangers and how to reduce them to a minimum. Talk to your partner about how to assess the risks of using a Bunsen burner to boil some water. Think about what might go wrong and how to prevent accidents. Compare your ideas with those of another group and see how many ideas you have in common.

Did You Know...?

Some chemicals are used by artists to etch patterns on metal and glass. The artists must take safety precautions to protect themselves, just like scientists in a laboratory.

Hazard warning signs

BIG IDEAS

You are learning to:
- Recognise warning signs
- Decide how to protect yourself from hazards
- Locate and use safety information from hazcards

Hazard symbols in the laboratory

Laboratories are exciting places but they can be dangerous too. Some chemicals catch fire easily. We call them **flammable** materials. Others may be **toxic**. Toxic substances can harm you if you breathe them in or swallow them or even touch them.

FIGURE 1: Hazard-warning signs. Can you think why they don't have any writing on them? (Hint: imagine you were working in a laboratory in Russia and you didn't speak the language.)

Some materials can damage our environment, harming plants and animals. The hazard-warning signs are simple and clear.

1 Why do we need hazard-warning signs in science laboratories?

2 The chemical copper sulphate can be harmful. Look at the hazard-warning signs in Figure 1 and choose the best one for it.

How Science Works

Look at the warning signs in the photo. Explain to your partner the reason for each of them. Ask your partner to suggest one way to make it safe when you put petrol in a car's petrol tank.

Signs need to be quickly understood

One of the most hazardous chemicals in daily use is petrol. Car engines need a liquid fuel that vaporises and burns easily. In the wrong place, these same properties can cause a major hazard.

 Petroleum spirit Highly flammable   Do not eat or drink near the pump

 No smoking switch off engines   Only approved containers may be filled with petrol

 Switch off mobile or car telephones   Report promptly all spillages, however small, to site staff

 Pumps not to be used by persons under 16 years of age   Information on the safe use of petrol is displayed on the sales building or available on request

FIGURE 2: Fuels can be dangerous

... flammable

3 What hazard symbol would you choose for a car-windscreen cleaning liquid that contains alcohol?

4 Describe the hazard symbol that means 'material could damage plants'.

5 Why does it matter if different countries use different warning signs?

FIGURE 3: What do the hazard symbols on these bottles of household bleach and toilet cleaner tell you?

How Science Works

When we do practical work we need to check for any hazards before we start. We also need to know what to do if there is an accident, for example if a chemical is spilt. Even experienced scientists have accidents in the laboratory. This is why we have **Hazcards**. Hazcards are available on the Internet and as paper copies. This helps scientists check the risks of any new investigation and find out what to do if there is an accident.

Hazcards are very useful but they look complicated to use. Lots of students grow beautiful blue copper sulphate crystals (some students may have even grown them at home using 'crystal kits' bought in shops). However not all students realise the dangers of using this common chemical.

CLEAPSS

STUDENT SAFETY SHEETS 27

Copper and its compounds

including **Copper oxides, sulphate, chloride, nitrate, carbonate**

Substance	Hazard	Comment
Copper (metal)	LOW HAZARD	
Copper oxides cuprous *or* cupric oxide	☒ HARMFUL	Harmful if swallowed; dust irritates lungs and eyes.
Copper sulphate or **nitrate** solid *or* concentrated solutions (*1 M or more*)	☒ HARMFUL	Harmful if swallowed (especially saturated solutions for crystal-growing); solid may irritate eyes and skin. Water on anhydrous solid sulphate produces heat.
Copper sulphate or **nitrate** dilute solutions (*less than 1 M*)	LOW HAZARD	Benedict's solution and Fehling's solution both contain dilute copper sulphate but Fehling's solution has other hazards.
Copper carbonate solid (*malachite*)	☒ HARMFUL	Harmful if swallowed; dust irritates lungs and eyes.
Copper chloride solid *or* concentrated solutions (*1.4 M or more*)	☠ TOXIC	Toxic if swallowed; solid may irritate eyes and skin.
Copper chloride moderately dilute solutions (*less than 1.4 M but more than 0.15 M*)	☒ HARMFUL	Harmful if swallowed.
Copper chloride very dilute solutions (*less than 0.15 M*)	LOW HAZARD	

FIGURE 4: Part of the Hazcard that includes copper sulphate.

6 Imagine that you are going to grow your own blue crystals.
Which **two** problems can you see by reading the part of the Hazcard shown in Figure 4?

7 Identify the **three** least harmful substances on the Hazcard.

8 What happens to the temperature when anhydrous copper sulphate gets wet?

9 Name **three** substances that require you to have good eye protection.

The Bunsen burner

BIG IDEAS

You are learning to:
- Decide how to light a Bunsen burner
- Select the correct burner settings
- Plan how to work safely with a flame

The Bunsen burner

The first gas burners used gas made from coal. Today the Bunsen burner uses **natural gas** that has methane gas in it.

A rubber or plastic tube joins the tube connector to the gas tap. The burner can be controlled by:

- Changing the size of the flame by turning the gas tap.
- Changing the amount of air that mixes with the gas by sliding the collar over the air hole on the burner.

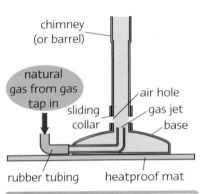

FIGURE 1: The Bunsen burner. Why is the burner on a heatproof mat?

Did You Know...?

Robert Bunsen was a German scientist (1811–1899) who needed a reliable way to heat things. He and other scientists experimented with many different burner designs before developing the Bunsen burner named after him.

1. What is the moveable part of a Bunsen burner called and what does it control?

2. Describe how a Bunsen flame changes if more air is allowed to mix with the gas.

Different flame colours

The Bunsen burner can burn with two colours of flame.

- The yellow Bunsen flame looks similar to a candle flame.
- The blue flame reminds us of a gas cooker or a gas barbecue burner.

The difference is caused by the amount of air that is mixed with the methane before it is burnt. This is controlled by the position of the sliding collar.

- The yellow flame is called a safety flame or **luminous** flame. It gives out lots of light and is easy to see.
- The blue flame is called a **non-luminous** flame. On a bright day the blue flame can be almost invisible.

3. Why is the sliding collar on a Bunsen burner also a safety feature?

4. Why does a Bunsen burner have a wide metal base?

5. The central blue cone in the blue flame is unburnt gas. Suggest how a scientist could prove this.

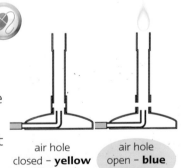

air hole closed – **yellow flame**   air hole open – **blue flame**

FIGURE 2: How a Bunsen burner flame changes when the air hole is open and shut. Why must you take extra care when the air hole is fully open on a bright day?

Getting to know your Bunsen burner

The table summarises the differences between the two types of Bunsen burner flames.

Yellow, luminous flame	Blue, non-luminous flame
closed air hole	open air hole
silent	makes a sound
leaves **soot**	no soot in the flame
wavy flame	flame has a regular shape
flame is less hot	flame is very hot

You are going to investigate how a Bunsen burner flame changes when the position of the sliding collar is changed.

Your teacher will provide you with the apparatus that you may need for your investigation.

Method:

1   Light your Bunsen burner — *always* light the Bunsen burner with the air hole closed. It is easier to light and it gives the safety flame.

2   Experiment with the gas pressure by turning the gas tap very slowly. Can you see the way the flame size changes?

3   Place the end of a metal spatula in the yellow flame for a few seconds and then look at the spatula. Note down in your notebook what you see.

4   Open the air hole completely by sliding the collar. Can you see the central blue cone and hear the sound?

How Science Works

Discuss with your partner how you would determine the key steps in using a Bunsen burner safely. Devise a short list of checks you would make when testing someone else. Decide how many of the test points you need to score before being awarded your Bunsen burner driving licence. HSW

Questions

1   Test yourself by naming all the parts of the Bunsen burner (*Hint:* use Figure 1 if you need help).

2   Why is it a bad idea to heat things with a luminous flame?

3   Why do you think that burning candles a lot makes the ceiling dirty?

4   Gas heaters always use a blue flame. Some heaters have a small ceramic rod that glows red in the flame. How might this idea be useful in the laboratory?

5   **a)** Why is the blue flame hotter?

   b) Why is air needed for a hot flame?

   c) Why is there no soot with a blue flame?

The best flame

BIG IDEAS

You are learning to:
- Identify the hottest part of the flame
- Explain what we mean by burning
- Evaluate the evidence for different flame temperatures

Glowing filaments

Old-fashioned light bulbs have a wire **filament** that glows white-hot. If you watch stage lights being switched on, they get brighter. The metal filament changes from red to white hot. A similar idea can be used to show how hot a Bunsen flame is. Not all parts of the flame are equally hot.

1 Where is the hottest part of the blue flame?

2 Explain what you can see with the lowest wire in Figure 2.

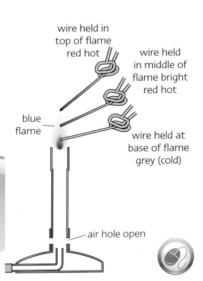

wire held in top of flame red hot

wire held in middle of flame bright red hot

blue flame

wire held at base of flame grey (cold)

air hole open

FIGURE 2: Three different wires were held one at a time in a blue Bunsen burner flame in three different parts of the flame — top, middle and at its base.

FIGURE 1: A light bulb showing the wire filament.

Comparing blue and yellow flames

If the Bunsen burner flame is yellow, the gas has not burnt completely. This is why carbon particles (**soot**) are left over. It is these particles that make the flame luminous. Heating with a yellow flame covers the apparatus in black soot. It is also wasteful because less heat energy is given out by a yellow flame.

The scientific name for burning is **combustion**.

- In a blue flame, combustion is **complete**.
- The yellow flame is an example of **incomplete** combustion — a wire held in a yellow flame glows less brightly.

3 Explain what 'combustion' means.

4 Describe how the temperature of different flames could be investigated using wires.

5 Why is a yellow flame an example of incomplete combustion?

... combustion ... complete

Burning a candle

You are going to observe closely what happens when a candle burns. Your teacher will place a floating candle in a bowl of water, and then carefully light it. Once alight, a glass jar will be placed on top to see what happens next once the candle's air supply is limited.

Questions

1. Predict what will happen to the candle when the jar is placed on top.

2. Observe any changes to the candle and to the water levels both inside and outside the jar.

3. Explain your observations.

4. Devise one improvement to the experiment that would allow you to take some relevant measurements.

... fire triangle ... fuel ... oxygen

Putting out a fire

BIG IDEAS

Your are learning to:
- Explain why carbon dioxide is used in extinguishers
- Select the correct extinguisher for a fire
- Explain the kinds of decisions fire-fighters must take

Gas fire extinguishers

The gas called **carbon dioxide** is much heavier (more dense) than air. Carbon dioxide stops air reaching a fire and so the fire goes out. This is a much safer way of putting out electrical fires than using water.

Soda-acid fire extinguishers also rely on carbon dioxide gas. When the two separate chemicals inside mix together, the carbon dioxide released forces out the water on to the fire. This type of extinguisher cannot be used for electrical fires since water is released.

1 Use the fire triangle on page 58 to explain how a soda-acid extinguisher puts out a fire.

2 Why is a soda-acid fire extinguisher unsafe to use on a burning television?

3 Suggest why a colour code is used for different kinds of fire extinguisher.

Did You Know...?

The 'eternal flames' in the Middle East are mysterious flames that just seem to escape from the ground. They are called the 'eternal flames'.
It used to be thought they were magic but it is now known that the flames are really burning natural gas leaking out from underground deposits, perhaps set on fire by lightning.

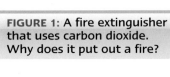
FIGURE 1: A fire extinguisher that uses carbon dioxide. Why does it put out a fire?

What to do if there is a fire

Pouring water over a burning electrical device is very dangerous. The water can conduct electricity and give you an electric shock. Cutting off the air supply is one possible solution. Some fire extinguishers work like this. Most homes do not have a fire extinguisher.

4 This man has called for the fire-fighters. What should he do to control the fire before they arrive?

5 Which is the correct action, fighting a fire yourself or warning others and leaving a burning room?

... carbon dioxide ... dry-powder fire extinguisher

Foam and fire blankets

There is a problem with burning oil. Oil is less dense than water and floats to the top. If you pour water on to burning oil it carries on burning. Aircraft carry enormous amounts of fuel in their wings. If an aircraft has an accident, terrible fires can break out. **Foam** is less dense than the burning oil and so it lies on top of the oil and cuts off the air supply.

At home, you can put out a burning pan of oil by covering it with a damp cloth. Some people have special **fire blankets** in the kitchen or in their car.

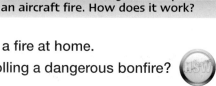

FIGURE 2: Foam being used to put out an aircraft fire. How does it work?

6 a) Explain, using your knowledge of the properties of foams, why it is suitable to put out oil fires.

b) Give several factors that might influence the spread of a fire at home.

c) What precautions should fire fighters take when controlling a dangerous bonfire?

Dry-powder fire extinguishers

Sometimes a fire can occur in a car engine. These fires are very dangerous since they can spread quickly and the fuel in the tank may explode. Some cars are fitted with **dry-powder extinguishers**. The powder is sprayed over the fire and stops oxygen getting to it.

7 To put out a burning car engine fire-fighters must first open the bonnet. Why is this a problem?

8 When might you use a dry-powder extinguisher at home?

How Science Works

On 5th November, large bonfires are built, often in unsuitable places. Some people include old car tyres in their bonfires, even though they release toxic fumes when they burn.

FIGURE 3: In December 2005 an oil storage depot in Hertfordshire caught fire. Fire crews brought the fire under control as quickly as possible but a cloud of pollution hung over the area for several days after.

9 Give **three** factors that might affect a decision to build an oil storage depot near a town.

... fire blanket ... foam ... soda-acid fire extinguisher

Fire precautions at school

BIG IDEAS

Your are learning to:
- Decide why fire precautions are important
- Use a model fire extinguisher to demonstrate how it works

Fire at school

Fire damage may close a school. Fire-fighters can spend many hours trying to control a major fire. Luckily most fires at schools start when the schools are closed. When the fire has been put out a **forensic scientist** can try to find out exactly how the fire began. Fires can spread quickly once they start.

1 What is the worst time of day for a school fire to break out?

2 Give **one** example of something you might notice if a fire has started.

Did You Know...?

Some of the doors in your school will be fire doors. These are specially designed heavy fire-resistant doors with self-closing hinges. They often have the following warning sign on them.

Fire door Keep closed

Fire precautions

Do you know about the fire precautions at your school? Every classroom should have most of the following things.

- Fire notice — tells you what to do if you discover a fire. It also gives you the route to follow to leave the building safely.
- Green fire exit sign with an arrow showing the direction to take when you leave.
- Fire blanket with pictures explaining how to use it.
- Fire extinguishers filled with carbon dioxide or with a mixture that produces foam.

Fire Door Do Not Block

Fire Assembly Point ✓

Fire exit

Keep clear !

FIGURE 1: All these notices give people advice in the event of a fire. They can save lives.

Outside the room there may be a **fire alarm** where you break the glass to set off an alarm. Fire notices and arrows are often coloured red and yellow and are **luminous** (glows in the dark). Once safely outside the building, students go to the **assembly point** where registers are read.

3 Why is it important that all students understand the fire precautions in their school?

4 Which gas is often helpful in putting out fires?

5 Why are luminous signs especially useful in fires?

How Science Works

Slow-burning fuses are used in fireworks to give people time to stand back after lighting a firework.

They are made by soaking paper or fabric in a special chemical called potassium nitrate. When it dries, it burns in a slow and controlled way.

Making a model fire extinguisher

The most common type of fire extinguisher is a soda-acid extinguisher. It contains a carbonate and an acid. When carbonates react with acids, a gas is produced.

> Acid + carbonate ➔ a salt
> + water + carbon dioxide gas

This is what happens inside the soda-acid extinguisher. The two chemicals are kept apart inside the extinguisher until it is used. On mixing, the gas pressure forces out a stream of water and foam to put out the fire.

Method:

1 Measure 50cm^3 dilute hydrochloric acid into a 250cm^3 conical flask.

2 Add a little washing-up liquid to produce foam.

3 Put some dry sodium bicarbonate into a small test tube. Tie a thread round the top of the tube and lower it into the flask. Keep the open end above the acid.

4 Seal the flask with a stopper fitted with a short plastic tube.

5 Light a small candle in an empty tray.

6 Tip the flask to mix the soda and acid and direct the spray on to the candle flame.

Questions

1 Explain why the contents of the flask do not react straight away.

2 In what way is a real soda acid extinguisher different to the model?

3 What are the safety hazards with this experiment? Find a Hazcard that offers some relevant advice.

Acids and alkalis

BIG IDEAS

You are learning to:
- Sort common materials into acids and alkalis
- Explain some properties of acids and alkalis
- Recognise the common chemical properties of acids and alkalis

Acids are sour!

How would you describe the taste of vinegar or lemon juice? The first word you probably think of is '**sour**'. They taste sour because they have a chemical in them called an **acid**.

- Vinegar contains ethanoic acid.
- Lemon juice contains citric acid.

Acids are often found in foods.

Washing soda is a useful cleaning material used in the home. It removes grease and helps to unblock drains. It has a chemical in it called an **alkali** and it is **soapy** when touched.

1 What properties of vinegar might tell you it contains an acid?

2 How do we use washing soda at home?

3 Why do bottles of oven cleaner have safety labels?

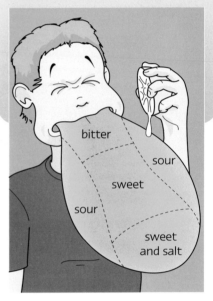

Did You Know...?

You 'taste' different foods with different parts of your tongue. You 'taste' chemicals that give a feeling of 'sour' down the sides of your tongue.

Hazard-warning signs

Acids and alkalis can be dangerous. There are usually warning signs on many products that contain acids or alkalis. They are called hazard-warning signs.

- **Corrosive** hazard-warning sign — this means the product can attack and destroy living tissues, for example the skin and eyes.

- **Irritant** hazard-warning sign — this means the product is not corrosive but it is likely to redden and blister the skin.

4 What precautions should you take when using corrosive materials in the laboratory?

5 Why is a hazard-warning sign on a bottle of cleaning material better than a written warning?

What is an acid?

All acids have the element **hydrogen** in them.
Three acids often used in the laboratory are:

- sulphuric acid, H_2SO_4
- nitric acid, HNO_3
- hydrochloric acid, HCl.

These three acids are called **mineral acids**. Can you think where in your digestive system there is an acid? It is in your stomach — the acid is called hydrochloric acid and it helps to digest the food that you eat.

Other acids, such as citric acid in lemons and ethanoic acid in vinegar are called **organic acids**. Fresh milk contains a sugar called lactose. When milk goes sour lactose turns into an organic acid called lactic acid.

Concentrated fruit squash is usually diluted with water before it is drunk. An acid that is concentrated can also be diluted by adding water. It is safer to use dilute acids rather than concentrated ones.

FIGURE 3: Common acids. What element is in all acids?

6 Is it true that all acids contain oxygen? Explain your answer.

7 Suggest why there is no hazard-warning sign on a lemon.

FIGURE 4: Common alkalis. What particle is in all alkalis?

Common alkalis

All alkalis have particles called **hydroxides** in them.

Three alkalis often used in the laboratory are:

- sodium hydroxide, NaOH
- potassium hydroxide, KOH
- calcium hydroxide, $Ca(OH)_2$.

A solution of ammonia (sometimes called ammonium hydroxide) is also used as an alkali in the laboratory.

In the kitchen there are other alkalis such as bicarbonate of soda (its chemical name is sodium hydrogencarbonate). Some medicines such as Milk of magnesia also contain alkalis.

8 What do most of the chemical names of the laboratory alkalis above have in common?

9 What information would be useful to you in deciding which oven cleaner would be safe for a child to use?

The M6 motorway near Stafford was closed earlier today after a tanker carrying 20 tonnes of highly acidic sulphuric acid started to leak some of its contents. The motorway remained closed for four hours whilst the fire brigade cleared up the spillage.

Have you seen road tankers similar to this one on any of your journeys? Tankers like this may be transporting all sorts of chemicals to customers.

On the sides and back of every road tanker there are large orange signs that give information about the load the tanker is carrying.

Fire-fighters and other accident and emergency service workers are trained to read these signs quickly so they can react to an accident immediately.

This label gives information that was used by fire-fighters and police when the acid spilled on the motorway.

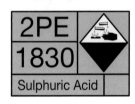

2PE
1830
Sulphuric Acid

After any incident a record is kept.

Incident number	Date	Location	Dangerous goods involved	Incident details
W16/01	17/5/01	M6 Between Stafford and Stoke (J14 and 15)	Sulphuric acid	Approximately 150 litres of acid leaked on to the road from a loose pipe on the tanker. The acid was diluted and no injuries were reported. No damage to road surface.

Before road tankers, concentrated sulphuric acid was transported in large glass bottles called carboys. These were tightly sealed and packed in a steel cage with plenty of straw.

Assess Yourself

1 Much of the sulphuric acid used in the UK is imported. Why is it transported in road tankers and not by train?

2 Why were carboys more dangerous for transporting concentrated sulphuric acid?

3 What are the possible hazards of these road tankers?

4 What are the advantages of labels on road tankers following a road accident in which the driver of the tanker is unconscious?

5 Mr Singh uses sulphuric acid in his factory. He only uses about 20 litres each month. He prefers the carboys he used to be able to buy rather than a tanker delivery. Suggest why.

6 Look at the report on the accident on the motorway. How was the spillage of sulphuric acid treated? Suggest why reports of this type are important.

7 On the orange label on the tanker there is a hazard sign. What does it mean?

8 A large spillage of concentrated sulphuric acid occurs close to a small brook. What must the emergency services avoid if at all possible?

9 The information on the label can be understood if you use the Hazchem Code. Can you find out how to solve the Hazchem Code?

Maths Activity

Road tankers deliver petrol and diesel to local garages. Find out what volume of fuel a tanker holds. Then calculate the number of motorists that could buy 20 litres of fuel from one tanker load.

Level Booster

8 You can analyse the potential problems of transporting hazardous materials and suggest what action to take in an emergency. You can rationalise your advice using published safety information.

7 You can analyse how decisions about transporting hazardous materials are taken and how they can be justified in terms of the Hazchem Code information.

6 You can explain how hazardous materials are transported using your knowledge of the Hazchem Code. You can justify the steps taken by fire-fighters after an accident.

5 You can explain how care must be taken in transporting some chemicals and the consequences of an accident.

4 You can describe the way chemicals are moved on the roads and how special safety signs are shown to warn people of the dangers.

Indicators

BIG IDEAS

You are learning to:
- Describe how indicators can be used
- Explain how an indicator can be extracted from a plant
- Identify acids and alkalis using the evidence from indicators

Indicators

Have you ever stood waiting for a train? You may have seen a screen that tells you how long you have to wait. This is called an **indicator** board. It shows you something.

In Science we use substances called indicators to show us something.

Some indicators are used to detect **acids** and **alkalis**. An example of an indicator is **litmus**. It can be bought either as a **solution** or as strips of paper soaked in the dye. These are called **litmus papers**.

Litmus paper turns red when it is in an acid and blue when it is in an alkali.

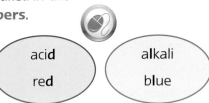

acid — red

alkali — blue

FIGURE 1: The indicator screen shows the people when they are allowed to get on to their train.

1 Look at figure 2. Has the litmus solution been added to an acid or an alkali?

2 Look at figure 3. Each piece of litmus paper has been dipped in a beaker. Which beakers had acids in them and which alkalis.

Did You Know...?

An alkali such as sodium hydroxide can do even more damage to a person's skin than sulphuric acid.

FIGURE 2: Acid or alkali?

Being neutral

If red and blue litmus papers are added to pure water, the red litmus paper stays red and the blue litmus paper stays blue. Pure water is not an acid and is not an alkali. Pure water is described as **neutral**.

We can make indicators for acids and alkalis using different plant materials such as red cabbage, beetroot and certain types of flower.

3 Frances dips a piece of red and a piece of blue litmus paper into pure water. What colours do they turn?

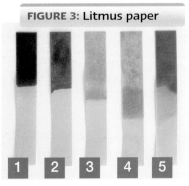

FIGURE 3: Litmus paper

1 2 3 4 5

Making your own indicator

There are lots of ways that indicators can be helpful to us in everyday life.

- Indicator paper is fixed to tree trunks to test for acid-rain pollution.
- The water leaking out of landfill sites can become polluted. Indicators are used to test the water to see if there are harmful acids or alkalis in it.

You are going to make your own indicator using leaves from the red cabbage plant.

Your teacher will provide you with the apparatus that you may need for your investigation.

Method:

1   Heat about 300 cm³ of water in the larger beaker until the water is boiling. Turn off the gas supply to put out the Bunsen burner flame.

2   Put about 5 cm³ depth of shredded red cabbage into the boiling tube and just cover it with ethanol.

3   Warm the mixture by dipping the boiling tube into the beaker of hot water. Extra ethanol can be added if needed.

4   Filter the solution into the small beaker to remove the remains of red cabbage.

5   Divide the solution into four portions by pouring it into the test tubes.

6   Use the marker pen to label your test tubes **1** to **4**.

7   Add different things to each test tube as listed below and note the change in colour:

- test tube 1: add an equal volume of dilute sulphuric acid (an acid)
- test tube 2: add an equal volume of dilute sodium hydroxide solution (an alkali)
- test tube 3: add an equal volume of solution **X**
- test tube 4: add an equal volume of solution **Y**.

8   Copy the following table into your notebook and record your results in it.

Test tube number	Substance added	Colour change
1	dilute sulphuric acid	
2	dilute sodium hydroxide solution	
3	X	
4	Y	

Questions

1   What colour does red cabbage solution turn in acid?

2   What colour does red cabbage solution turn in alkali?

3   Is solution **X** an acid or an alkali?

4   Is solution **Y** an acid or an alkali?

5   How good was the method you used to extract the indicator? Discuss with your partner what improvements could be made.

Weak and strong

BIG IDEAS

You are learning to:
- Recognise that acids can be weak or strong
- Explain the differences between weak and strong
- Make connections between the strength and the pH

Acid on your chips

You may put vinegar on your chips but you would not put sulphuric acid on them!

- Both acids turn blue **litmus** red but vinegar is a **weak acid** and sulphuric acid is a **strong acid**. Sulphuric acid can cause severe burns.

- Bicarbonate of soda is a **weak alkali** used in indigestion powders. Sodium hydroxide is a **strong alkali** used to strip paint off doors and to clear blocked drains.

1 Write down the names of:
a a strong acid
b a weak acid.

2 Write down the names of:
a a strong alkali
b a weak alkali.

FIGURE 1: Sodium hydroxide is very corrosive. What is it being used for here?

Measuring the strength of an acid or an alkali

The strength of an acid or alkali can be measured using a mixture of indicators called **Universal indicator**. Universal indicator changes colour when the acidity or alkalinity of a solution changes. Each colour is given a different **pH number**.

STRONG ACIDS	1	
	2	
	3	red
	4	
WEAK ACIDS	5	orange
	6	yellow
NEUTRAL	7	green
WEAK ALKALIS	8	blue
	9	blue-purple
	10	
	11	
	12	purple
	13	
	14	

FIGURE 2: The pH colour chart. Can you suggest what pH value an alkali household cleaner might have?

3 **a** A few drops of Universal indicator are added to a beaker half-full of pure water. The colour changes to green. Using the pH colour chart shown in Figure 2, what is the pH value of water?
b Is pure water acid, alkaline or neutral?

Did You Know...?

- Litmus is a 'single indicator' – it gives colours for acid, alkali and **neutral**.
- Universal indicator is made by mixing together lots of indicators. This is why it gives lots of different colours.

... litmus ... neutral ... pH number ... strong acid

4 A sample of rainwater is tested with Universal indicator. Look at the photograph. What does this tell you about rainwater?

5 Suggest why it is difficult to find the pH value of blackcurrant juice using Universal indicator.

Strong *versus* concentrated

It is a common mistake to confuse 'strong' with 'concentrated' and 'weak' with 'dilute'.

As we have seen strong and weak refer to the pH of an acid or an alkali.

- A solution with a low pH value is a strong acid.
- A solution with a high pH value is a strong alkali.

The concentration of an acid or alkali refers to how much water it contains.

- A concentrated acid or alkali contains little or no water.
- A dilute acid is made by adding water to a concentrated acid.

FIGURE 3: Rainwater goes yellow with universal indicator.

6 Dilute hydrochloric acid has a pH value of 1.
  a What colour does Universal indicator turn in dilute hydrochloric acid?
  b Is dilute hydrochloric acid a strong acid or a weak acid?

7 Nitric acid is a strong acid. Some nitric acid is added to a large volume of water.

Which one of the following statements is true about the solution formed?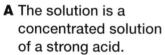
  A The solution is a concentrated solution of a strong acid.
  B The solution is a dilute solution of a strong acid.
  C The solution is a concentrated solution of a weak acid.
  D The solution is a dilute solution of a weak acid.

8 What are the risks of testing unknown solutions and how might you manage these risks?

How Science Works

Use the pH table when you test a variety of solutions with pH indicator (universal indicator). First test as many of the chemicals named as possible. Next test some unlabelled solutions and sort them into weak or strong categories.

Substance	pH	Acid or alkaline?
hydrochloric, nitric and sulphuric acids, car battery acid	0–1	strongly acidic
phosphoric acid	1–2	acidic
citrus fruit, e.g. lemons, oranges, vinegar	4	acidic
distilled water	7	neutral
egg, handsoap	8	alkaline
ammonia	11	alkaline
oven cleaner	12	alkaline
caustic soda, paint strippers	13–14	strongly alkaline

HSW

The pH meter

BIG IDEAS

You are learning to:

- Describe how we use a pH meter
- Interpret the pH meter scale
- Provide evidence for reliable pH values

Measuring pH

Farmers and gardeners sometimes want to check the **pH value** of their soils. Plants grow better in soils that have a suitable pH.

Some plants produce different coloured flowers when they are grown in soil with a different pH value. The flowers are acting like the plant's own indicator. They show us that the soil pH can change in different parts of the country.

FIGURE 1: Measuring the pH value of soil using a pH meter. The probe is pushed into the soil and the pH value is read on the meter scale.

Farmers and gardeners can buy strips of Universal indicator paper to measure the pH of their soils. Or they can buy a simple meter called a **pH meter** that measures the pH value of the soil directly.

1 Which would give a more sensitive pH reading: a universal indicator or a pH meter?

Did You Know...?

In hilly country you can find peat bogs full of dead plant material. These peat bogs are acidic if you test them with indicator. The acid conditions preserves things – including the bodies of people from the Iron Age!

pH meters in use

Scientists use pH meters when they have a lot of pH values to measure. This could be in or out of the laboratory. It is also useful if a scientist wishes to watch how the pH value in an investigation changes over time. This is called **monitoring** the pH.

2 What are the advantages and the disadvantages of using a pH meter rather than using Universal indicator paper in a laboratory investigation?

FIGURE 2: A scientist is monitoring the pH value of a solution over time. What instrument is he using to do this?

How Science Works

Whenever you eat, a mixture of food and bacteria starts to build up on your teeth. This layer is called plaque. The bacteria produce acids that attack the enamel covering on teeth. This is why our toothpastes contain an alkali – to neutralise the harmful acids made by the bacteria, and to help reduce the damage done to the protective enamel layer.

... buffer solution ... calibrate ... monitoring

Setting up and using a pH meter

A group of students are carrying out a survey on a stream to find out how many different kinds of creatures live in the water. They take a portable pH meter with them to measure the pH of the water.

When there is pollution of water, for example by acids, there are changes in the types and numbers of organisms living in the water.

You are going to set up and use a pH meter to investigate the pH value of different solutions.

Your teacher will provide you with the apparatus that you may need for your investigation.

Method:

1   Collect the solution of known pH value. This is called a **buffer solution**.

    You need to use this to set up (**calibrate**) your pH meter.

2   Dip the probe into solutions **W**, **X**, **Y** and **Z** in turn. Wash the probe thoroughly with distilled water and dry it in between dippings.

3   Record the pH value of each solution in a table in your notebook using the following headings.

Solution	pH value

Questions

1   Write down the solutions in order starting with the most acidic and finishing with the most alkaline.

2   Why must the probe be washed in distilled water in between dippings?

3   Why should you not use water from the tap to wash the probe?

4   How can you use a pH meter to find out the impact of water pollution?

Neutralisation

BIG IDEAS

You are learning to:
- Describe how acids and alkalis can cancel each other out
- Interpret neutralisation in terms of particles
- Demonstrate the pH colour changes during neutralisation

Going into battle

There is a battle going on here, shown in figure 1. At the end of the battle, the two sides have cancelled each other out. It is a bit like this when **acids** and **alkalis** join together. All acids contain hydrogen particles (H). All alkalis contain hydroxide particles (OH). When they join up we get HOH that we write as H_2O, water.

FIGURE 1: Fighting it out. Is there a winner?

Neutralisation takes place when acids cancel out alkalis. If we mix an acid and an alkali in the correct amounts a **neutral** solution is formed.

1 What is likely to happen if there are more soldiers with 'H' than with 'OH' in the battle?

pH value and neutralisation

Neutralisation takes place when the correct amounts of acid and alkali are mixed.

2 You have **four** solutions with the following pH values:

solution **P**, pH 1   solution **Q**, pH 4   solution **R**, pH 7   solution **S**, pH 10

Which of the following pairs could produce a neutral solution when mixed together?

P and **Q**   **P** and **R**   **Q** and **S**   **R** and **S**

3 Mandy spills some dilute hydrochloric acid on the bench. The teacher asks her to clear it up by neutralising the acid. Suggest a substance she might use safely to do this.

Planning an investigation

A scientist has to plan an investigation carefully before they carry it out. They have to be sure that the investigation is **fair** and that they take all of the results they need.

- If a scientist takes just one reading and makes a mistake, they are unlikely to spot an error.
- If they take a lot of results, they will see a pattern in their data. A result that is simply wrong will now be easier to spot and they can check it again.
- They must also monitor their vats of dye continually to make sure the pH is within the correct range and if it is not, correct it by adding something that neutralises too much acid or alkali.

4 Laura is told that when neutralisation takes place heat energy is given out. She wants to devise an investigation to show this. What steps should she take in making her plan?

... acid ... alkali ... fair

Science in Practice

Now for a neutralisation!

Cloth can be given many different colours by using dyes. The pH of the dye and water mixture can change the colour of the finished fabric. Dyers experiment with changing the pH by adding washing soda (alkaline) or white vinegar (acidic).

You are going to neutralise an alkaline solution using acid and an indicator.

Your teacher will provide you with the apparatus that you may need for your investigation.

Method:

1 Use a measuring cylinder to transfer 25cm³ of dilute sodium hydroxide solution into a conical flask. Add a few drops of Universal indicator solution using a pipette.

2 Write down the colour of the solution in your notebook.

3 Fill a burette with dilute hydrochloric acid.

4 Add the acid slowly to the flask, shaking the solution gently as you do it.

5 Try to stop the process when the solution is neutral (the solution turns green). It isn't easy! You might have to try several times before you are successful.

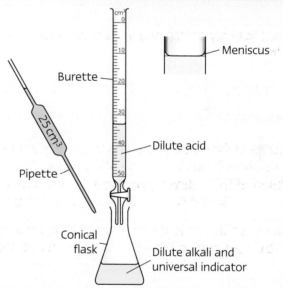

Questions

1 Discuss possible ways of neutralising the alkali.

2 Why is it difficult to make the solution exactly neutral?

3 What did you do to try to improve your method each time?

4 Write a detailed plan of an investigation to show that when neutralisation takes place, heat energy is given out. Show it to your teacher. It may be possible to carry out your plan.

Neutralisation in action

BIG IDEAS

You are learning to:
- Recognise some everyday examples of neutralisation
- Discuss how alkaline materials are used to treat an acid stomach
- Explain how neutralisation can improve the environment

Have you ever eaten sherbet?

If you have, you have carried out a **neutralisation** reaction in your mouth.

Sherbet contains an acid (citric acid) and a weak alkali (bicarbonate of soda). When the mixture gets wet in your mouth, a reaction takes place. You feel fizzing in your mouth. The alkali neutralises the acid, and bubbles of **carbon dioxide** are formed. It is these bubbles that give you the fizzing feeling.

Neutralisation reactions take place in some other substances that we use.

- Toothpaste is usually slightly alkaline. This is to neutralise acidity in the mouth that can damage the outer enamel layer of teeth. Some toothpastes contain bicarbonate of soda.

- Indigestion tablets may be taken by a person suffering from indigestion. They take away the pain. The stomach contains hydrochloric acid to digest food. Indigestion can occur when there is too much acid in the stomach. Indigestion tablets may contain one or more weak alkalis. When a tablet is swallowed the alkalis in it neutralise the excess acidity in the stomach.

FIGURE 1: What type of reaction takes place when we use these products?

1 Look at the label from an indigestion medicine (right). Which **three** alkalis do the tablets contain?

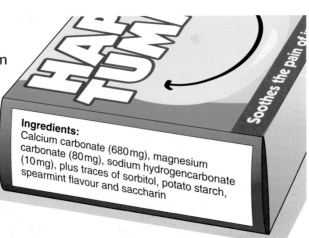

Ingredients:
Calcium carbonate (680 mg), magnesium carbonate (80 mg), sodium hydrogencarbonate (10 mg), plus traces of sorbitol, potato starch, spearmint flavour and saccharin

2 At first indigestion medicines were made as powders. The instructions said 'take two spoonfuls of powder'. Suggest why tablets are better.

How Science Works

Test small samples of toothpastes and gels with pH indicator. Add an indigestion tablet to a tube of boiling water that contains 5 drops of acid and some universal indicator. Explain the effect of the tablet on the colour of this solution.

... acid rain ... calcium carbonate ... carbon dioxide

FIGURE 2: Why is this farmer spreading lime on to his field?

Using alkalis

The soil in farmers' fields can become increasingly acidic over time. Lime (an alkali) is spread on the fields to neutralise the acidity. Lime is made from a rock called limestone.

When coal is burnt in a coal-fired power station it forms some sulphur dioxide gas. This is acidic and can cause acid rain. The sulphur dioxide is removed from the waste gases as it passes up the chimney by reacting it with an alkali called calcium carbonate.

Not all of the sulphur can be removed but there is a great reduction in air pollution.

Did You Know...?

We call pure limestone by a different name, it is the white rock called chalk.
Both limestone and chalk were formed under the sea millions of years ago. Earth movements have brought the rocks back above sea level so they can be used.

3   A small lake is found to be very acidic and it is causing the fish to die. Suggest what could be done to reduce the acidity of the lake.

4   Why does a power-station owner prefer to buy low-sulphur coal even if it is more expensive than ordinary coal?

FIGURE 3: How are the levels of sulphur dioxide kept low in this coal-fired power station?

1. For each of the following statements write 'T' if the statement is true or 'F' if it is false.

   A A liquid that can burn is flammable.

   B Water is a flammable liquid.

   C Heat is given out when something burns.

   D A luminous gas flame is a very hot flame.

   E A Bunsen burner is adjusted by turning the collar.

2. The table below gives the pH values of soil at which certain vegetables and fruit grow best.

pH 5.2	pH 6.0	pH 6.7	pH 7.5
bilberry	broad beans	asparagus	asparagus
cranberry	gooseberry	broad beans	broccoli
gooseberry	peas	broccoli	cabbage
potato	potato	cabbage	peas
strawberries	strawberries	peas	sugarbeet

   From the table, which fruit or vegetable can only be grown in a pH:

   a less than 6.0   b greater than 7.0   c 6.0 to 7.5?

3. Match the symbol letter with its correct name.

   Hazchem symbols: **Name:**

   A   toxic

   B   corrosive

   C   flammable

   D   harmful

4. Methanol is a liquid used as an anti-freeze in cars. It is mixed with water and used in windscreen wash bottles.

   a Why does the label include hazard symbols?

   b What does anti-freeze liquid do?

   a What **two** safety precautions must you take when using this anti-freeze liquid?

5 A road tanker is carrying a chemical called sodium hydroxide solution.

   a Which hazard-warning sign should be on the tanker?

      corrosive   flammable   oxidising

   b If the chemical is spilled on to the road, fire-fighters know how to neutralise it. Suggest what substance they could use to do this.

6 Sophie heated water in a beaker using a Bunsen burner. She measured the temperature of the water every 2 minutes. Here are her results.

Temperature (°C)	22	30	45	60	75	95	100	100
Time (mins)	0	2	4	6	8	10	12	14

   a What is the pattern shown by the data in the table?

   b Why do the temperature readings start at 22 °C?

   c How soon was the highest temperature reached?

   d Why did the temperature stop rising?

7 What type of fire extinguisher, or other method, would you choose for each fire? Explain your choice.

   a Burning paper that is inside a metal waste bin.

   b Burning chip fat in a pan on an electric hob.

   c Burning oil around a damaged car.

   d Burning clothing on a person near a Bunsen burner.

8 Tariq and Mohammed carry out an investigation. They measure the pH values as they add different volumes of dilute hydrochloric acid to 25 cm^3 of sodium hydroxide solution. The diagram shows the apparatus they use. The graph shows their results.

   a Name the piece of apparatus labelled **X**.

   b What volume of hydrochloric acid exactly neutralises 25 cm^3 of sodium hydroxide? How did you find this out from the graph?

   c They repeated the experiment but added the same sodium hydroxide solution to 25 cm^3 of hydrochloric acid in the flask. What volume of sodium hydroxide is needed to exactly neutralise 25 cm^3 of hydrochloric acid?

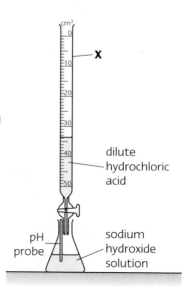

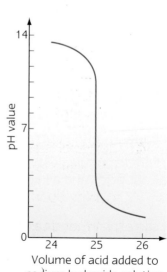

Volume of acid added to sodium hydroxide solution

Topic Summary

Learning Checklist

4

☆ I know the meaning of some safety signs. — Page 52

☆ I know the meaning of 'combustion'. — Page 56

☆ I can draw a bar graph.

☆ I know that wasps and bees inject chemicals when they sting. — Page 64

☆ I know that there are natural acids and alkalis. — Page 64

5

☆ I know the meaning of most safety signs. — Page 52

☆ I can interpret the data on a bar graph.

☆ I can explain the fire triangle in terms of combustion. — Page 64

☆ I can list different types of fire extinguishers. — Page 60

☆ I know that wasp stings are alkaline. — Page 64

☆ I know that bee stings are acidic. — Page 64

☆ I know the names of three mineral acids. — Page 64

☆ I know that indicators can identify acids and alkalis. — Page 68

☆ I know that indigestion medicines rely on neutralisation. — Page 76

☆ I know how to use a pH meter. — Page 70

6

☆ I know how to use Hazcards. — Page 52

☆ I know the importance of oxygen in combustion. — Page 58

☆ I can spot errors (anomalies) in data on a bar graph.

☆ I know the limitations of using water to put out fires. — Page 60

☆ I can choose the correct extinguisher for a fire. — Page 60

☆ I know how stings may be neutralised. — Page 64

☆ I know the colours produced by indicators such as litmus and red cabbage. — Page 68

☆ I know the difference between strong and weak acids and alkalis. — Page 64

☆ I understand the importance of hazard signs on chemical tankers. — Page 52

7

☆ I know how to apply the information in Hazcards. — Page 52

☆ I can explain temperature rise in terms of the particle model. — Page 58

☆ I know that in neutralisation, hydrogen from acids reacts with hydroxide from alkalis. — Page 74

☆ I can distinguish between strong and concentrated, dilute and weak when talking about acids and alkalis. — Page 64

☆ I can explain combustion in terms of oxidation — Page 58

☆ I can write and explain formulae equations for neutralisation — Page 74

☆ I can give examples of exothermic and endothermic reactions — Page 58

80

Topic Quiz

1 What do we mean by hazards?

2 What are the two colours of a Bunsen burner flame?

3 Why shouldn't you heat alcohol over a gas flame?

4 What are the labels on the fire triangle?

5 What sorts of fires should not be put out using water?

6 How do students know the safe route to leave a room in a fire drill?

7 Which is the stronger acid, one with a pH value of 1 or a pH value of 5?

8 What colour is litmus when in an acid?

9 Would an indigestion remedy have a pH value above or below 7?

True or False?

If a statement is false then rewrite it so it is correct.

1 Water is flammable.

2 A blue flame is hotter than a yellow flame.

3 Foam is no use to put out oil fires.

4 Ethanoic acid is a weak acid.

5 Some plants and flowers give dyes that are used as indicators.

6 pH meters give more precise readings of pH than indicator paper.

7 The treatment for wasp stings is vinegar.

Numeracy Activity

The table below shows how long different beakers of water took to start boiling when heated. Draw a bar graph using the information. The same Bunsen burner was used each time.

Beaker	Time to boil (mins)
A	10
B	5
C	12
D	15
E	8

● What can you tell from the bar graph?

● Why do you think that the results for different beakers are not all the same?

Literacy Activity

Choose **five** keywords from pages 58 to 63 about fires and fire precautions. Write a short story about a school fire. Include the five keywords in your story. Explain the lessons that can be learned from what happened in your story.

COMBUSTION

Fireworks are perfect examples of chemical reactions. There are sparks, bright colours, movement and sound. There are lots of different energy changes that take place when a firework burns. The chemical energy can make rockets fly, Catherine wheels spin and mortars explode high in the air.

Fireworks have a long history. The famous 'Greek fire' (a deadly mixture of chemicals that caught fire spontaneously when thrown) used in the ancient world was a terrifying weapon of war.

Have you noticed that fireworks burn away quickly? In fact they burn so fast that there often isn't time for air to get in and help the burning to continue. It is for this reason that fireworks have special chemicals inside them that give them the oxygen they need. Oxygen is the active gas in the air.

Explosive chemicals have been used throughout history. You already know about the 5th November 1605 when Guy Fawkes was arrested just before he could demonstrate the power of gunpowder. The black powder he put under the Houses of Parliament in the hope of blowing them up used a very old recipe.

FRANKLYN'S CIGARETTES

ARREST OF GUY FAWKES

Particles and Reactions

What special colouring chemicals went into these fireworks?

Chinese scientists had developed gunpowder by the 9th Century.

Gunpowder only has three chemicals in it — charcoal, sulphur and saltpetre. The trick is to get the amounts just right so that the mixture explodes! Many fireworks used today still use gunpowder. The special colours of fireworks are made by adding extra chemicals. For example, copper compounds give blue, sodium compounds give yellow and strontium compounds give a deep dark-red.

What do you know?

1 Name **two** different kinds of fireworks.

2 How many changes might you see when a rocket is lit?

3 How can you change the colour of a firework?

4 Give **one** example of firework chemicals being used to fight a battle.

5 Why should you always put the lid back on a box of fireworks?

6 How many times can you burn a firework?

7 Describe **two** energy changes that occur in fireworks.

8 Why do sailors often carry rocket flares on their boats?

9 What was the name of the first known explosive mixture of chemicals?

10 Why do fireworks need chemicals that contain their own oxygen?

Particle world

BIG IDEAS

You are learning to:
- Describe how everything is made of particles
- Classify the ways that particles are arranged
- Explain the ways that particles behave

Particle line-up

In a sports stadium people are arranged close together in rows. There is a clear **pattern** to their arrangement.

- In a **solid** tiny **particles** are also arranged in a regular pattern. The particles are also in **contact** with each other.

When a solid such as ice is heated, it melts. The particles are all still there but now they can move around.

- In a **liquid** the particles are still touching but they can also slide past each other.

FIGURE 1: Patterns occur when people are sat in rows.

If you have ever filled a balloon with water and then squeezed it, you will know about liquids. Since the particles in liquids are touching, there are no spaces in between them. Squeezing the balloon just makes it burst and you get wet.

- In a **gas** there are spaces in between the particles. Squeezing just pushes the particles closer. You can **compress** gases but not solids or liquids.

1 How are the particles arranged in a solid?

2 Why can a liquid not be compressed?

3 Describe what happens to the particles on the surface of a liquid as it evaporates.

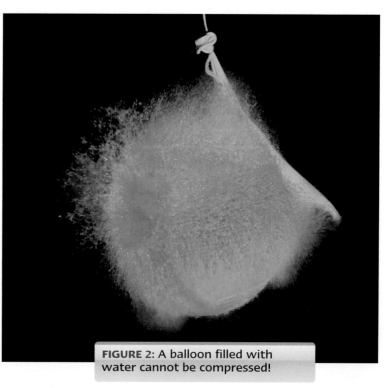

FIGURE 2: A balloon filled with water cannot be compressed!

... *compress ... contact ... force ... gas ... liquid*

Using the properties of liquids

When the brake pedal in a car is pressed down by the driver's foot, a liquid is pushed along a pipe until it reaches the brakes. The **force** of the person's foot puts the brakes on. The force from the foot is **transmitted** through the liquid. If liquids behaved like gases the liquid in the brakes system would compress and then the brakes would not go on!

4 What kind of material fills the brake pipes in cars?

5 Suggest why the brakes on a car should be checked regularly.

6 What would happen if some air leaked into the brake pipe? Explain your answer.

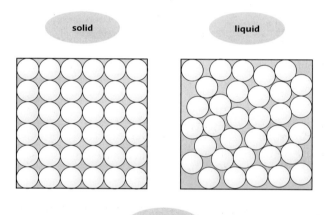

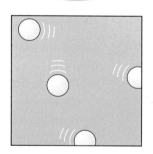

FIGURE 3: The arrangement of particles in a solid, a liquid and a gas. Why can a solid not be compressed?

How Science Works

How could you use marbles to model the arrangement of particles in solids, liquids and gases? What features would this model show? What would it *not* show? See if you can find an animation on the internet showing the arrangement of particles in solids, liquids and gases. What is good about it? And what does it not show?

Did You Know...?

When you let down a bicycle tyre the escaping air feels cold. The particles use up their energy in escaping and spreading out, which causes a cooling effect.

7 Explain, in terms of particles, what happens when steam condenses on a cold mirror.

Our watery world

BIG IDEAS

You are learning to:
- Describe changes of state
- Define changes of state
- Explain the link between energy and changes of state

Naming the changes

- In Figure 2 the **liquid** water on the road is turning into a **gas**. The energy needed for this change of **state** comes from the Sun. The process is called **evaporation**. You see the reverse of this change when you breathe on a cold mirror. This process is called **condensation**.

- If you put orange juice in a beaker in the freezer to make an ice-lolly it sets solid. This change from liquid to solid is called **freezing**. Energy is taken away from the orange until it sets **solid**. If you leave the ice-lolly out on the kitchen table, it warms up and turns back into a liquid. This is called **melting**.

1 Name the **three** states of water.

2 Does melting ice take in heat or give out heat?

3 **a** How could you use a bottle taken from the fridge to show that there is water vapour in the air?
 b When particles in a liquid gain heat, what changes occur?
 c Why does it feel so painful when particles in steam condense on your skin?

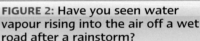
FIGURE 1: The 'blue planet'. Earth seen from space.

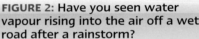
FIGURE 2: Have you seen water vapour rising into the air off a wet road after a rainstorm?

How Science Works

These are examples of changes of state:
- A kettle boiling and releasing steam
- Holding a cold metal baking tray in the jet of steam
- Lighting a candle then pouring liquid wax on to cold glass

How many changes of state can you identify and name? Describe in terms of particles what happens to the wax particles in the candle experiment.

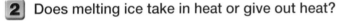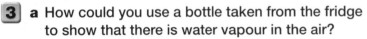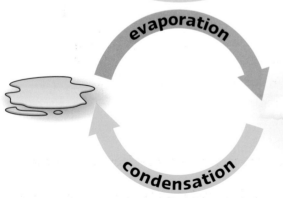

Heat energy is gained by particles

evaporation

condensation

Heat energy is lost by particles

FIGURE 3: Evaporation and condensation are reversible reactions. How do we know this?

Physical or chemical change?

- Changes of state are all examples of **physical changes**. In a physical change no new material that has new properties is formed. It is usually quite easy to reverse a physical change.

- In **chemical changes** new materials are formed that are quite different from the reactants. Chemical changes are normally irreversible.

4 State whether each of these is a physical or a chemical change:
  a heating chocolate over boiling water
  b pouring hot wax into cold water
  c evaporating sea water to leave salt
  d burning a firework
  e heating an ice cube with a hair dryer
  f leaving an iron nail in the rain to go rusty

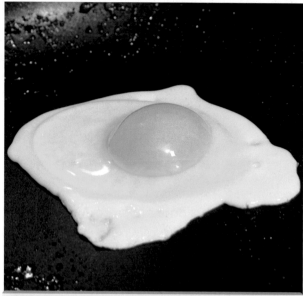

FIGURE 4: Is cooking an egg a chemical change or a physical change?

How Science Works

The 'Mars effect'

Studies of Mars by space probes show that it has a very thin atmosphere made up almost totally of carbon dioxide (it is estimated that the atmosphere is 95% carbon dioxide). Carbon dioxide is a solid at low temperatures but exists as a gas at higher temperatures, as on Earth.

The orbit of Mars is not a perfect circle around the Sun so that sometimes it comes closer to Earth than normal. When it does, it becomes clear that the planet has a strong red colour over almost all of its surface. Telescopes show that Mars sometimes has white patches on its surface in two different polar areas. They are thought to be a mixture made mainly of frozen carbon dioxide (called 'dry ice'). During the Martian summer these polar patches disappear again.

FIGURE 5: Mars is sometimes called the 'red planet'. You can clearly see the white areas over the poles.

5 Explain the seasonal changes seen on the surface of Mars in terms of changes of state.

6 Burning hydrogen gas in air gives steam, which turns into water drops then ice on a very cold surface. Identify all the physical and chemical changes here.

... gas ... liquid ... melting ... physical change ... solid

Spreading out

BIG IDEAS

You are learning to:
- Describe how particles can spread out
- Explain these changes

Spreading evidence

If you put a coin on a saucer, it stays there. If you put a drop of perfume or nail polish remover on a saucer, it disappears. The ways that the particles in the coin and in the perfume are behaving are different. The particles in a perfume spread out. The name for this spreading out is **diffusion**. This is why you can smell perfume from a distance. The liquid perfume first **evaporates** and then the particles of perfume gas diffuse through the air and reach your nose.

FIGURE 1: In what way is this woman using diffusion?

Did You Know...?

If you spill a bottle of perfume on the pavement, the particles can spread in the air right round the world.
If you yawn, the particles can spread in the air to the other side of the planet.

1 How does diffusion tell you dinner is cooking when you are in another room?

2 How can diffusion help you discover a fire?

Colours in liquids

Some solutions have strong colours. **Copper sulphate** solution is blue. If the blue solution is put in a tall glass jar and a layer of clear water carefully added on top, something strange happens. Even without stirring, the colour slowly moves. After some hours, still without stirring, the colour is the same everywhere. This is diffusion in a liquid and it is slower than in gases.

The behaviour of particles in different materials is called the **particle theory**.

3 Why are coloured liquids good for diffusion experiments?

4 Which is faster, diffusion in liquids or in gases?

5 Use the particle theory to explain your answer to **Q4**.

FIGURE 2: Diffusion in a liquid. Why does the colour spread evenly throughout the glass jar?

... copper sulphate ... diffusion

How fast is diffusion?

Carrying out diffusion experiments with gases is difficult because most gases are invisible and diffusion in gases takes place rapidly. It is better to study diffusion in liquids because many solutions are coloured.

Universal indicator turns red in acid. If some pellets of a solid alkali are dropped into a glass cylinder of acid and Universal indicator, the alkali falls to the base and starts to dissolve, producing a pattern of colour bands. The alkali spreads upwards by diffusion. Unfortunately the beautiful effect is temporary; diffusion continues for the next few days, mixing up all the colour bands. You are going to investigate the speed at which different chemicals diffuse. Your teacher will provide you with the apparatus that you may need for your investigation.

FIGURE 3: These colour bands are temporary because of diffusion.

Method:

1 Choose three tall glass cylinders.

2 Pour 1 cm of each coloured liquid into a test tube — one colour in each tube.

3 Very carefully add water on top of the coloured liquid in each test tube, using a dropper. Be careful not to let the layers mix.

4 Put an elastic band around the test tube at the level of the coloured liquid.

5 Place the test tubes in a test tube rack without letting the liquids mix.

6 Observe the speed of diffusion as the colour moves over the next two days.

7 Copy the table below into your notebook and record your results.

Sample	Colour after 1 day	Colour after 2 days	Colour after 3 days

Questions

1 Which colour diffused fastest?

2 Did the strength of the colour change?

3 How could you use this investigation to obtain data for a graph?

4 Describe **one** way in which diffusion might help to solve a crime.

How does heat change things?

BIG IDEAS

You are learning to:
- Investigate how heat changes some materials
- Explain how some of these changes can be reversed

Forest fire

When a forest fire breaks out, the effects can be terrible. Wildlife is destroyed or driven out by the flames and heat. When the fire is over, the forest looks completely different. The trees and green plants that lived there are turned into charcoal, ash and smoke. We have to wait years and years for new plants to grow to replace the old forest.

Many **chemical changes** are like this — they are not **reversible**. Burning a firework or birthday candles are also **irreversible** changes – we cannot go back to the start again.

FIGURE 1: Effects of forest fires.

1 What do we mean by 'reversible change'?

2 What changes do you see when a candle burns?

Going backwards

There are many examples of reversible changes.

- A recipe may start by melting some fat or butter in a pan. If butter is heated it changes from a **solid** to a **liquid** — it **melts**. When the heat is switched off the melted butter cools down and turns back into a solid again.
- Snow or ice melts to water. Cooling the water turns it back into ice again.
- If you breathe on to a mirror you see mist on the glass. Wait a few moments and the mist disappears again.

3 Explain how breathing on glass is an example of a reversible change.

4 Name **one** reversible change when a candle burns.

5 Is baking bread a reversible change? Explain your answer.

FIGURE 2: Cooking is all about changing. Is butter melting a reversible change?

Did You Know...?

In 2002 Arizona suffered its worst ever forest fire. The fire raged out of control for almost three weeks, engulfing several communities, before being brought under control by specially trained forest fire-fighters. The fire destroyed 1890 km² of forest.

... chemical change ... irreversible ... liquid ... melt

Heating and changing

Glass bottles break easily if you drop them but glass can be heated until it becomes liquid. It is a sticky liquid, a bit like treacle. Molten glass can be moulded into shape, as with bottles for milk or for perfume. On cooling, the glass turns back into its normal solid state.

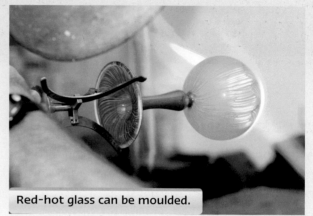

Red-hot glass can be moulded.

The heat from a Bunsen burner flame is enough to cause many changes. Some substances melt, others catch fire and some don't change at all.

You are going to use your observation skills to see if a change is really reversible.

Your teacher will provide you with the apparatus that you may need for your investigation.

Method:

1   Put a wooden splint in a shallow metal dish and cover it with sand.

2   Put a second splint on top of the sand.

3   Heat the dish very strongly over a blue Bunsen burner flame for 10 minutes.

4   Switch off the Bunsen burner and leave the dish to cool.

5   Compare the two wooden splints. Make a note of your observations in your notebook.

6   Switch on the Bunsen burner again (*Remember:* always light the Bunsen with its safety flame at first). Heat some wax carefully in a test tube. Make a note in your notebook of any changes that you see on heating and on cooling the wax.

7   Copy the table below into your notebook and record your results.

Investigation	Reversible or not?
wood under sand	
wood on top of sand	
wax	

Questions

1   How were the results different for the two splints?

2   Why were the results different?

3   Identify **one** reversible change. Explain your choice.

4   What happened to the sand on heating?

5   Describe the different ways that chocolate changes if you heat it over boiling water or over a Bunsen flame.

How does the mass change?

BIG IDEAS

You are learning to:
- Describe how we measure mass
- Explain how small mass changes can be measured
- Develop your observation skills

Crystal surprises

You can grow beautiful blue **crystals** using a chemical called copper sulphate solution. (You may have grown these at home using a crystal kit from a shop.) The blue solution is also used in vineyards. By spraying the growing vines with a weak solution of copper sulphate, it is possible to kill off any mould that would damage the grapes that are used to make wine. Particles in crystals are arranged in regular 3-D patterns. In ordinary salt, the particles have the shape of a cube, we call it a cubic crystal structure.

FIGURE 1: Beautiful crystals can be grown from a solution of copper sulphate.

Copper sulphate crystals look and feel completely dry but they contain a secret. Inside every crystal is some water. Without this water their colour would be different. You can investigate this change in colour in the practical on the facing page.

1 Give **two** uses of copper sulphate.

2 What is the 'secret' of copper sulphate crystals?

FIGURE 2: Inside a salt crystal.

'Flash' chemistry

When magnesium in the form of a wire or a ribbon burns, it produces a brilliant white light and leaves behind a white ash. If you weigh the magnesium at the start and the ash at the end you find something interesting.

The magnesium is weighed and then it is burned in a small heat-proof container called a **crucible**.

Here are the results of one student's experiment.

	At start	After heating	Change in mass
Mass of crucible and magnesium (g)	17.52	17.82	0.30

FIGURE 3: Photography in the early days used a magnesium flashgun and involved lots of smoke!

3 What happens to the mass when magnesium burns?

4 What is the active gas in air called?

5 What might the ash produced in the investigation contain in addition to the magnesium?

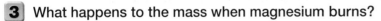

... crucible ... crystal

Changing crystals by heating

The decimal system is based on the number ten. Sodium carbonate <u>deca</u>hydrate is a solid that contains ten lots of water for one of the chemical. When you open a new packet of this chemical, the crystals look clear and glassy. If the packet is left open for a week everything changes. The chemical turns into a white powder because most of its **water of crystallisation** has escaped into the air. This changes the appearance of the crystals.

We know that copper sulphate crystals contain some water so it may be possible to change the crystals by heating them.

You are going to investigate the effect of heat on crystals of copper sulphate. Follow the instructions carefully so that you don't miss some of the changes!

Your teacher will provide you with the apparatus that you may need for your investigation.

Did You Know...?

When you buy something such as a camera you often find a tiny fabric bag inside, filled with crystals. These are silica gel and they absorb moisture to keep your camera dry.

Method:

1   Using the spatula put copper sulphate crystals into a dry tube to a depth of 2 cm.

2   Clamp the tube so that the open end is just a little lower than the closed end — so that it is *almost* lying flat.

3   Heat the crystals gently using a Bunsen burner.

4   Note any observations you make in your notebook.

5   Turn off the Bunsen burner.

6   When the apparatus is cold, remove the tube.

7   Add a few drops of water very slowly and note your observations in your notebook.

8   Copy the table below into your notebook and record your results.

Observations of copper sulphate crystals before heating	
Observations of copper sulphate crystals during heating	
Observations of copper sulphate crystals on adding drops of water	

Questions

1   Suggest why the apparatus needs to be set up with the tube slightly sloping.

2   What is the material that collects near the open end of the tube?

3   How many colour changes occur during the investigation?

4   Describe **two** changes that occur when a few drops of water are added to the cooled material.

5   Washing soda crystals lose water of crystallisation to the air. They change from clear glassy crystals to a dull white powder. How could you find out exactly how much water was lost by the crystals?

David Hempleman-Adams has broken another world record for the highest altitude reached in a hot air balloon. The record the British adventurer set has broken the previous highest hot air balloon altitude record of 32 300 feet by 200 feet. The previous record had been unbroken for 27 years.

Mr Hempleman-Adams wore an oxygen mask and a parachute as he broke the record. The temperatures in Alberta, Canada, where the flight took place, dropped as low as –60°C. As the balloon rose, some pieces of Mr Hempleman-Adams' equipment started to fail due to the cold conditions. He had to deal with his oxygen mask, VHF radio and GPS navigation system freezing, and at one stage the propane burner went out. Mr Hempleman-Adams was delighted when he completed his challenge, but said there had been problems. "It was a very hard landing", he said, "But I am pleased to have done it".

Mr Hempleman-Adams has made history before. He was the first person to fly a balloon over the North Pole in 2000, and in 2003 he became the first person to cross the Atlantic Ocean in a balloon with an open wicker basket. He became the first man in history to reach the Geographic and Magnetic North and South Poles, as well as climb the highest peaks in all seven continents – a feat he has named the Adventurers' Grand Slam.

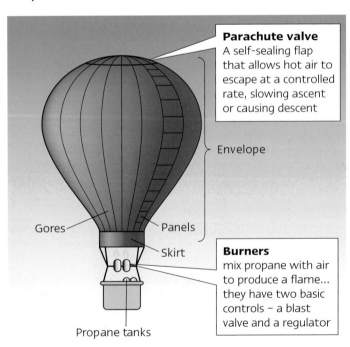

Parachute valve
A self-sealing flap that allows hot air to escape at a controlled rate, slowing ascent or causing descent

Envelope

Gores

Panels

Skirt

Burners
mix propane with air to produce a flame... they have two basic controls – a blast valve and a regulator

Propane tanks

How a hot air balloon works

1) First, the pilot opens the valve on the propane cylinder and lights the burner.

2) Then the balloon starts to fill with gas and expand

3) When the balloon is full of hot air, the balloon and the basket start to lift off the ground.

4) When the balloon is high up and floating in the air, every so often the pilot turns up the burners again to 'top up' the envelope with hot air.

Assess Yourself

1 Draw particle diagrams to show a solid, a liquid and a gas.

2 Give an example of a solid, a liquid and a gas that might be found in a hot air balloon.

3 Explain, using ideas about particles and respiration, why David Hempleman-Adams needed an oxygen mask to fly at high altitude.

4 How can you tell if a chemical reaction has taken place? Give an example of where you can see a chemical reaction take place when a hot air balloon flies.

5 Draw particle models of the propane gas when it is a liquid in the cylinder, and the gas as it comes out of the burner. Use a particle diagram to show how the propane might react with a gas in the air.

6 Using your knowledge of the chemical reaction for burning, explain why the propane burner might have gone out at high altitude.

7 Using your knowledge of particles, and a diagram to support your explanation, describe the arrangement of the particles on the inside and the outside of the hot air balloon and explain how this helps the balloon to float.

Numeracy activity

Use the data in the table to make a prediction about what volume of envelope would be needed to carry 15 people, and 40 people in a balloon. (Hint: it will help if you draw a graph.)

Number of people the balloon is designed to carry	Volume of envelope (m^3)
One	Less than 1 000
Four	2 500
Twenty-four	15 000

ICT Activity

Summarise the phlogiston theory as on-screen bullet points. Compare your own summary with a partner to see which is clearer.

Level Booster

8 You can explain in detail, using ideas about energy, forces and particles, why hot air balloons have less lift at very high altitudes.

7 You can link what you know about energy, particles and forces to explain why the amount of 'lift' from a hot air balloon depends on the external temperature of the air outside the balloon.

6 You can also: use the term 'density' to explain why the balloon filled with hot air rises, and support your explanation with particle diagrams of each stage of the process.

5 You can also explain how the arrangement of the particles inside and outside the balloon helps to make it fly.

4 You can correctly draw and label particle diagrams for a solid, liquid and gas, and give examples of each.

BIG IDEAS

You are learning to:
- Describe changes that you see
- Explain changes
- Interpret the features of a chemical reaction

Chemical reactions

What changes in a chemical reaction?

When water turns into ice and then melts again, nothing new has been made. **Chemical reactions** are different. New materials are always made in chemical reactions. We often notice heat changes, colour changes, or even fizzing.

1 Why isn't melting ice an example of a chemical reaction?

2 Name **two** different changes you might see in a chemical reaction.

FIGURE 1: Chemical changes can be fun.

How do we know it is a chemical reaction?

A person with indigestion may take Seltzer tablets. The tablets contain **alkalis** that help reduce the amount of **acid** in the person's stomach. We know that a chemical reaction is taking place by **observing** the following:

- The tablet fizzes and breaks up into small pieces if it is dropped into a glass of water.
- A very sensitive thermometer measures a small change in temperature of the water as the tablet breaks up.

These observations are clues that a chemical reaction has taken place in the water. The following are things to look for when deciding if a chemical reaction has taken place:

- a change in temperature
- a colour change
- a gas or gases being produced
- a change in mass
- light being given out.

3 How many changes are there when a Seltzer tablet is added to water?

4 **a** How can you tell if a gas is given off in the reaction of a Seltzer tablet with water?
b What change would you notice here if you had your eyes closed?
c How can you show that the temperature has changed?

5 Are chemical reactions usually reversible?

Did You Know...?

Many rocks look similar to each other. To identify some of them scientists put a few drops of acid onto them. If the rocks fizz they are limestone.

FIGURE 2: A Seltzer tablet in a glass of water. Can you see any bubbles?

... acid ... alkali ... chemical reaction

Model volcano reactions

The chemistry of volcanoes is very complex and still not fully understood. However, there is a laboratory chemical that burns in a way that can **model** a volcanic eruption.

The orange powder is first piled up in the shape of a volcano. When it burns there are many changes that indicate a chemical reaction has taken place.

FIGURE 4: A model volcano. What observations can you make?

At the start	Observations on burning
orange powder	green powder of larger volume produced
	steam, gas, sparks, heat produced

The green powder produced once the model volcano has stopped burning is toxic.

6 In what ways is the model volcano like a real erupting volcano?

7 What evidence can you find in the table above to indicate a chemical reaction?

8 Suggest why this reaction should not be carried out in an open room near to students.

9 Pale-coloured dust can reflect the light. How might pale-coloured volcanic dust in the atmosphere affect the amount of sunlight reaching the Earth?

FIGURE 3: Are there chemical reactions going on in this erupting volcano? How do you know?

Did You Know...?

The Sakurajima Volcano in Japan lies near to a city that has a population of 500 000 people. Because of this the volcano is monitored continually to try to predict when an eruption is going to happen.

Scientists know that the following observations indicate an eruption is likely:

● The temperature of nearby hot springs rises.
● Groundwater levels begin to rise.
● The chemical make-up and the amount of toxic gases released by the volcano change. The levels of sulphur dioxide released increase dramatically.

Fizzy reactions

BIG IDEAS

You are learning to:
- Describe a fizzy reaction
- Explain the changes in fizzy reactions
- State the names of some gases

Fizzy reactions

Some chemical reactions produce a gas as one of the **products**.

The scientific name for fizzing is **effervescence**.

- Metals such as zinc or magnesium effervesce when put into an acid. The gas inside the bubbles given off is very light. It is **hydrogen** gas. Hydrogen gas was once used to fill airships. Unfortunately hydrogen is very flammable (see page 104).

- Pieces of chalk, marble or limestone effervesce when put into an acid. The gas given off is **carbon dioxide**. Carbon dioxide is released from volcanoes and when fuels burn in air.

1 What does 'effervesce' mean?

2 Hydrogen and carbon dioxide cannot be seen. How could you use a wooden splint and a flame to identify each of these gases?

3 Name **three** rocks that effervesce in an acid.

How Science Works

Observe what happens when pieces of zinc metal are added to a beaker of acid. All acids contain hydrogen particles. How many different changes can you observe? What gas is produced? What useful evidence might a thermometer provide in this experiment?

Did You Know...?

The gas fizzing inside this **geyser** forces water high into the air. The gas may just be steam.

... carbon dioxide ... catalyst ... effervescence

Did You Know...?

You have a **catalyst** in every living cell in your body called catalase. It is an enzyme that speeds up the break down of harmful waste products to harmless substances. There is catalase in your blood.
The action of this enzyme can be demonstrated by putting a drop of blood into some hydrogen peroxide in a test tube – there is a lot of effervescence and a gas is produced that re-lights a glowing splint. Suggest what the active gas might be.

The 'life gas'

All living organisms need to breathe **oxygen** gas to stay alive. This is why it is sometimes called the 'life gas'.

Space scientists use oxygen in an interesting way. They use a chemical substance called hydrogen peroxide to help them power spacecraft. The chemical shorthand for hydrogen peroxide is H_2O_2. You can see by comparing the chemical shorthand for hydrogen peroxide and water (H_2O) that hydrogen peroxide contains more oxygen than water.

Inside the rockets in a spacecraft, hydrogen peroxide effervesces in a carefully controlled way so that oxygen is released at the correct rate to mix with the rocket fuel and burn.

FIGURE 1: 'We have lift off!' Why is hydrogen peroxide useful to space scientists?

4 Why do spacecraft need an internal oxygen supply?

5 How can you tell that there is more oxygen in hydrogen peroxide than in water?

6 What is the product when hydrogen and oxygen react?

7 How could you use a balloon and a balance to show that gases really do have a mass?

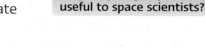

... *geyser ... hydrogen ... oxygen ... product*

More about burning

BIG IDEAS
You are learning to:
- Describe how the mass changes during burning
- Explain why mass changes on combustion
- Interpret the effects of combustion

A burning problem

- If a lit candle is left to **burn**, it gets smaller. The candle weighs *less* after burning than it did at the start.
- If magnesium is burnt it leaves a solid white ash which weighs *more* than the magnesium did at the start.

The problem is that burning seems to make some materials weigh less and other materials weigh more.

1 How could you check that the mass of the candle changes during burning?

2 What is the problem with understanding what happens when things burn?

FIGURE 1: What happens to the weight of a candle when it is left to burn?

Solving the problem

When magnesium burns it leaves a solid white ash. When a candle burns it produces the invisible gases water vapour and carbon dioxide. These gases have **mass**.

Figure 2 shows the apparatus used to burn a candle in a glass jar and trap the gases produced during the burning reaction. The gases are trapped by lumps of calcium chloride and soda lime lying on the wire **gauze**. The lumps **absorb** the gases and stop them escaping into the air. If the candle and its holder are weighed before and after burning, the mass increases just like magnesium.

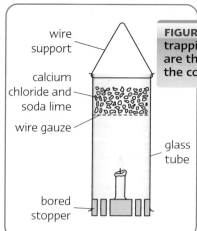

wire support
calcium chloride and soda lime
wire gauze
glass tube
bored stopper

FIGURE 2: Burning a candle in a glass jar and trapping the invisible gases produced. Why are the chemicals on the gauze high up in the container?

The mass always increases when a substance burns.

3 Why is it easier to weigh the product of burning magnesium rather than the products from a burning candle?

4 Suggest why there are holes in the base of the burning apparatus in Figure 2.

How Science Works

Early experimenters in chemistry used to ignore any gases that were produced during reactions. They could not think how to collect the gases to be able to study them.

Once this problem was solved by improved chemical technology, many new discoveries were made. This includes the importance of oxygen gas in burning.

... absorb ... burn

More burning reactions

A cutting torch uses pure oxygen instead of air. This makes the torch burn at a higher temperature — it is hot enough to melt steel. Some of the pieces of metal burn away as sparks.

You are going to investigate how different substances burn in air.

Your teacher will provide you with the apparatus that you may need for your investigation.

How Science Works

Oxyacetylene cutting torches are used to remove roofs of cars after a road accident. The temperature of the oxyacetylene flame is over 3000 °C and can cut through all metals.

Method:

1   Light your Bunsen burner with the safety flame and then open the air hole fully.

2   Hold a small sample of each substance in turn in metal tongs and burn it.

3   Observe the changes.

4   Copy the table below into your notebook and record your results.

Substance	Observed changes during burning
iron wool	
magnesium (1 cm strip)	
copper foil (1 cm strip)	
charcoal lump	
sugar cube	

Questions

1   Which substance melted in the flame?

2   Which material changed colour only?

3   Magnesium burns to give magnesium oxide. What is produced when iron burns?

4   Which materials burn the brightest?

5   Divers can light an oxyacetylene torch and then use the flame under water. How is this possible with no air available under water?

Everyday chemistry

BIG IDEAS

You are learning to:
- Describe everyday reactions
- Explain how many reactions are useful
- Explain why some chemical reactions cause problems

Sticking fast

Adhesives are chemical substances that are sticky. Sticky tape, paper glue and stamps are all examples of how we use adhesives.

- Some adhesives stick things together permanently such as wood glue.
- Other adhesives are not permanent — they can be peeled off again, such as labels or sticky notes. When you have your shoes heeled or stick a new hook in a cupboard, the special chemistry of adhesives is being used.

Cars are expensive to repair after an accident. Sometimes you can use **epoxy resin** to fill holes and dents, rather than buying a new part. A resin needs to be mixed with a second chemical before it sets hard. The liquid resin is mixed with a chemical **hardener** that starts the **chemical reaction**. The resin sets solid faster in warm weather.

1. What does 'adhesive' mean?

2. Give **two** examples of adhesives used in the home.

3. How could you speed up the time it takes for a resin to set?

Did You Know...?

The tiles on the space shuttle stop it burning up when returning to Earth from space. These tiles are held in place by a special heat-resistant adhesive.

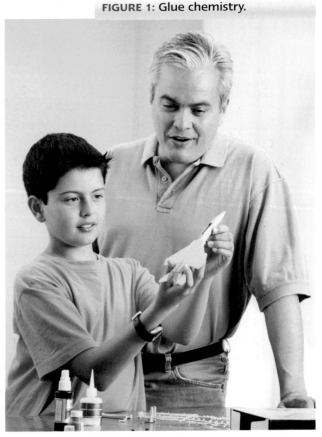

FIGURE 1: Glue chemistry.

FIGURE 2: Using epoxy resin filler to fill a dent in a car before it is re-painted.

... adhesive ... chemical reaction ... detergent

Clean chemistry

If your hands are dirty, washing them in plain water does not always work very well. Most dirt and grease is **insoluble** (does not dissolve) in water. **Soaps** and **detergents** are useful chemicals that are designed for cleaning. The particles in detergents have two different ends. One end likes to stick to dirt, the other end likes to stick to water. This loosens the dirt or grease and lets you remove it by washing.

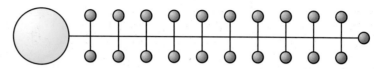

Head of the molecule is water-loving

Tail is water-hating but dissolves in grease and dirt

FIGURE 3: A detergent particle.

How Science Works

The large round end of the detergent particle (molecule) is attracted to water. The tail avoids water and sticks to grease and dirt instead. When the dirty clothes are moved around in the water, the dirt and grease are removed by the detergent and float away, surrounded by lots of detergent particles.

FIGURE 4: Chemistry helps to get you and your strip clean!

4 **a** Why do we need detergents?
   b What is unusual about detergent particles?
   c Why does hot water generally improve the cleaning power of detergents?

5 Suggest why clothes-washing machines move clothes around during a wash.

6 Give **one** example of something that probably would not be cleaned by a detergent.

7 The chemical reactions in your body work well at 37 °C, body temperature. Why do the makers of biological detergents advise you to use a washing temperature of about 40 °C?

Reactions running backwards

BIG IDEAS

You are learning to:
- Explain what we mean by reactants
- Explain what we mean by products
- Provide evidence that a change is permanent

Going with a 'bang'

Mixing some gases with air can cause an **explosion** if there is a spark. An example of this is petrol vapour at a petrol station.

Old airships used to be filled with hydrogen. This works well as long as the gas does not leak out. Mixtures of hydrogen and air are very dangerous. After hydrogen has exploded, something new and quite different is left.

hydrogen + oxygen = water, H_2O

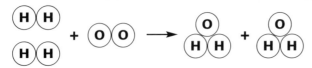

This chemical reaction can be **reversed**. When electricity is passed through water in a special apparatus, the water splits up again, giving hydrogen and oxygen. The hydrogen produced from water could be used as a clean fuel for cars. The only waste gas from the car exhaust would be steam.

Did You Know...?

In 1937 the German-built Hindenburge airship burst into flames while coming in to land in New Jersey.
The exact cause of the fire has never been agreed – but most people think that hydrogen gas leaked from one of the many cells on the airship and static electricity that had built up on the skin of the ship caused the gas to ignite and explode.

FIGURE 1: At petrol stations there are always no-smoking warning signs. Why is this?

1. Explain why coalminers make sure that they have no matches or lighters on them before they go down a mine. *Hint:* Many coalmines give off methane gas, the gas we use in Bunsen burners.

2. Why are modern airships filled with helium?

3. Describe how the reaction between hydrogen and oxygen can be reversed.

... explode ... irreversible

Surprising reactions

Mixing chemicals together can sometimes give surprising results. There can be colour changes, heat changes or bubbling. Most of these reactions are **irreversible**. The chemicals we start with are called the **reactants**. The materials left at the end of a reaction are called the **products**.

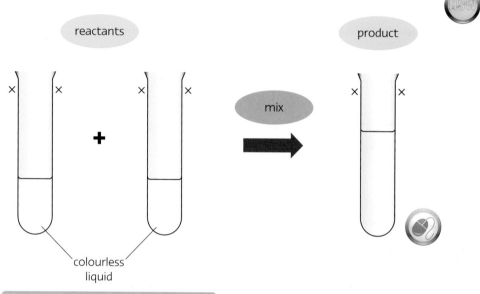

FIGURE 3: Mixing a surprise. Do you think this reaction is reversible?

Look at the descriptions of three different reactions in the table below. At the start, all of the materials are colourless.

Reaction	Substance 1	Substance 2	After mixing 1 and 2
A	potassium iodide solution	lead nitrate solution	turns yellow, lead iodide has formed
B	salt crystals	water	salty water
C	sodium sulphate solution	barium chloride solution	turns white, barium sulphate has formed

4 Which of the changes in the table is reversible?

5 Name the reactants in reaction **A**.

6 Name the product in reaction **C**.

7 The rusting of iron is usually irreversible. How do we stop iron bridges turning permanently into rust?

1 For each of the following statements write 'T' if the statement is true or 'F' if it is false.

    A Salt water dries to leave crystals.

    B Melting of butter can be reversed by cooling.

    C Melting ice is easier than melting butter at room temperature.

    D Bubbles contain nothing.

    E A Bunsen burner is adjusted by turning the collar.

2 Copy and complete the sentences using the words below. The words can be used once, more than once, or not at all.

    change   experiment   hydrogen   mixture   oxygen

    a Air is a_____ of different gases.

    b The active gas in air is_____ .

    c The gas needed for burning is_____ .

    d Burning is an energy_____ .

3 Write down each change and its correct description.

Change:	Description:
burning	physical change
freezing	chemical reaction
dissolving	chemical reaction
cooking food	physical change

4 Copy the table and choose the correct gas to match the description from the words below. You may use a word more than once.

    carbon dioxide   hydrogen   nitrogen   oxygen

Description of a use	Name of gas
A given off when magnesium is burnt	
B gives water when reacted with hydrogen	
C is in fizzy drinks	
D is in fire extinguishers	

5 What apparatus would you use for the following actions? Choose from the words below:

   bathroom scales   beaker   measuring cylinder
   chemical balance   measuring jug

   A Weighing about 2 kilos of flour.

   B Finding the volume of water that fills a test tube.

   C Finding the mass of one nail.

   D Measuring roughly, not accurately, 100 cm³ of water.

6 Some students weighed a piece of magnesium and then heated it. They collected the ash and weighed it again.

Sample	Student 1	Student 2
magnesium	0.35 g	0.35 g
ash	0.48 g	0.41 g

   a What happened to the mass on burning?

   b By how much did the mass change according to student 1?

   c Why did the mass change?

   d Suggest **one** reason why the results are different.

7 Explain **one** way to record the results of each experiment below and give **one** reason for your choice.

   A Monitoring the change in mass of a burning candle each minute for 10 minutes.

   B Recording the change in appearance of three different metals when burnt in oxygen.

8 There are three unlabelled solutions. One of the solutions contains an acid.

   a How could you use sodium carbonate powder to identify the solution that contains acid?

   b What would you expect to see?

Learning Checklist

☆ I know that things get dry in the Sun. page 86

☆ I know how to grow crystals. page 92

☆ I know that Seltzer tablets fizz in water. page 96

☆ I know some everyday examples of chemical reactions. page 102

☆ I know what is meant by reversible. page 104

☆ I can describe what happens in melting. page 90

☆ I can describe what happens in evaporation. page 90

☆ I know the difference between freezing and melting. page 90

☆ I know that some gas mixtures are explosive. page 96

☆ I know that changes can accompany chemical reactions. page 96

☆ I can explain what effervescence means. page 98

☆ I know what happens when magnesium burns. page 100

☆ I know about using adhesives. page 102

☆ I can recognise physical changes. page 86

☆ I know how mass changes in burning. page 92

☆ I can describe some examples of chemical reactions. page 96

☆ I know the part played by oxygen in burning. page 100

☆ I know why detergents are useful. page 102

☆ I know what is meant by an irreversible change. page 104

☆ I can describe changes of state in detail. page 86

☆ I know why mass increases on burning. page 92

☆ I know that geologists identify some rocks by their chemical reactions. page 96

☆ I know the risks associated with hydrogen. page 100

☆ I know that physical changes are often reversible. page 104

☆ I can name **three** common gases and know their tests. page 104

Topic Quiz

1 What happens when food burns?

2 What colour is the Earth from space?

3 What do we mean by a reversible reaction?

4 How can you get crystals from salt water?

5 Is cooking a reversible change?

6 What happens when water evaporates?

7 What do you see when a tablet effervesces?

8 Is freezing reversible or not?

9 Which gas in the air is needed for burning?

10 What happens to the mass of something when it burns?

11 What is meant by a 'change of state'?

12 How do geologists test limestone?

True or False?

If a statement is false then rewrite it so it is correct.

1 Forest fires allow new plants to grow.

2 Indigestion tablets contain an acid.

3 The freezing temperature and the melting temperature of water are different.

4 Magnesium burns in air to give a white ash.

5 Some things get lighter when they burn.

6 Burning is a physical change.

7 Hydrogen gas puts out flames.

8 'Water to water vapour' is an example of evaporation.

9 Physical changes are usually irreversible.

10 Many chemical reactions involve temperature changes.

11 All chemical reactions involve colour changes.

12 Water is the oxide of hydrogen.

Literacy Activity

Write a paragraph to describe what happens when a Seltzer tablet is added to a glass of water. Use the words below in your description.

changes   effervescence   gas   dissolve

ICT Activity

Make a glossary to explain the meanings of ten words of your choice in this unit. Set it out in a table with one column for each word and another for what the word means.

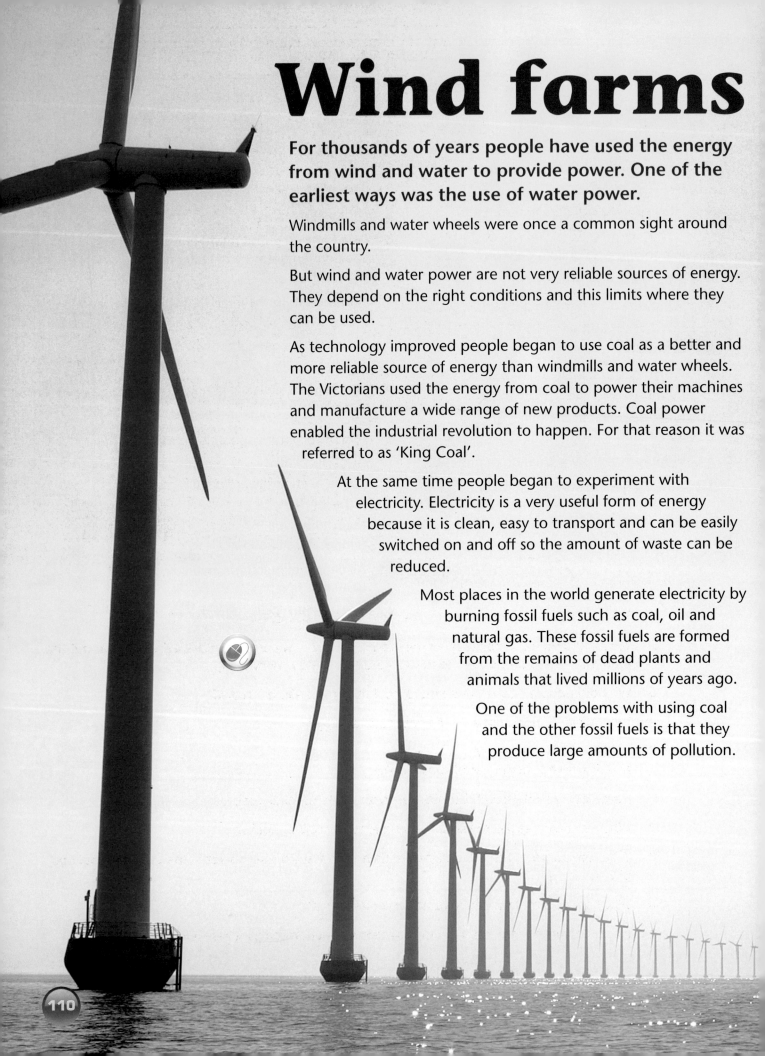

Wind farms

For thousands of years people have used the energy from wind and water to provide power. One of the earliest ways was the use of water power.

Windmills and water wheels were once a common sight around the country.

But wind and water power are not very reliable sources of energy. They depend on the right conditions and this limits where they can be used.

As technology improved people began to use coal as a better and more reliable source of energy than windmills and water wheels. The Victorians used the energy from coal to power their machines and manufacture a wide range of new products. Coal power enabled the industrial revolution to happen. For that reason it was referred to as 'King Coal'.

At the same time people began to experiment with electricity. Electricity is a very useful form of energy because it is clean, easy to transport and can be easily switched on and off so the amount of waste can be reduced.

Most places in the world generate electricity by burning fossil fuels such as coal, oil and natural gas. These fossil fuels are formed from the remains of dead plants and animals that lived millions of years ago.

One of the problems with using coal and the other fossil fuels is that they produce large amounts of pollution.

Recently; as the problems of pollution have got worse and supplies of fossil fuels begin to run out, people have begun to go back to using the energy in wind and water to generate electricity. As the technology has improved so these energy resources are beginning to be re-used.

Nowadays wind farms are a more common sight in our countryside and are also increasingly located out to sea.

Water power is being used to generate electricity at large power plants called hydroelectric plants. These use the energy in running water.

BIG IDEAS

By the end of this unit you will understand how energy can be transferred from one place to another. You will know more about the uses of fuels and why it is important to conserve them. You will be able to use the idea of energy transfer to explain what is happening in components in simple circuits. You will understand how scientific ideas can influence decisions about resources.

The Glen Canyon dam on the Colorado River in Arizona is the site of a hydroelectric power plant.

What do you know?

1 How was energy generated before the use of fossil fuels?

2 Why is it difficult to harness all the stored energy in wind and water? (*Hint:* think about the amount of wind and water needed to produce a little electricity).

3 Why did people begin to use more coal during the Victorian era?

4 Why is electricity such a useful source of energy?

5 a What is a fossil fuel?
  b Give **three** examples of fossil fuels.

6 Name **one** problem with burning large amounts of fossil fuels.

7 Why have we started to re-use wind and water power again?

8 What are some of the advantages of using wind and water power in the place of coal and oil?

9 What are some of the disadvantages of using oil?

10 How is electricity transported from where it is generated to where it is used?

Types of energy

BIG IDEAS

You are learning to:
- Describe how energy is measured
- Explain the effects of energy using the transformation model
- Describe the different forms of energy
- Recognise that energy can be thought of as having different forms

Energy makes things happen

One way to think about **energy** is to say that energy makes things happen. When a machine or an object moves or causes an event to happen it uses energy. Therefore without energy nothing would happen. Some things are useful because they can **store** energy.

- A battery stores energy. When it is connected to a device something happens.
- A wind-up radio stores energy. When it is wound up energy is put into it and when it unwinds energy is released and the radio plays.

1 What other things can you think of that store energy?

2 Suggest where the energy in a battery comes from.

Different forms of energy

Scientists often use models when they explain ideas. There are two ways of understanding energy: the transform model and the transfer model.

Energy is measured in **joules (J)**. The joule is named after the scientist James Joule (1818–1889) who did lots of experiments to discover more about energy.

This is a very small amount of energy. Food labels show how much energy is found in the different types of food that we eat. The amount of energy in the food is usually shown in **kilojoules (kJ)**. One kJ = 1000 joules.

A **calorie** is a unit of energy that is sometimes used instead of the joule. One calorie is equal to 4.2 joules.

The energy in food is in the form of stored energy. There are many other forms of energy:

- kinetic or moving energy, e.g. in a moving bullet
- heat, e.g. from a fire
- electrical energy, e.g. in an electric current
- chemical energy, e.g. stored in chemicals and batteries
- light energy, e.g. from the Sun
- sound energy, e.g. sound from a radio travels as a wave which contains energy

How Science Works

Light energy from the Sun is changed by plants into chemical energy. Humans gain this energy by eating plants or by eating animals that have fed on the plants. This chemical energy is changed into kinetic energy when the radio is wound up. The kinetic energy is changed into electrical energy to enable the radio to work. The radio changes it to heat, light and sound when it is switched on.

One joule is the amount of energy needed to heat 1 cm³ of water by 1°C.

... calorie ... energy ...

- nuclear energy, e.g. energy in the nuclei of atoms is released during a nuclear bomb explosion
- potential or stored energy, e.g. a bungee jump where a store of energy is released to make something happen
- gravitational potential energy, e.g. a person on a trampoline at the top of their bounce, where their energy is due to their height.

FIGURE 1: Food labels show the energy content of foods. Which has the higher energy value – the pasta or the sweetcorn? Is this what you expected?

PETRA'S Pasta Shapes

Nutritional Information

Typical values (per 100g serving) dry weight

ENERGY	1515KJ/357Kcal
PROTEIN	12.3g
CARBOHYDRATE	73.1g
OF WHICH SUGARS	3.5g
OF WHICH STARCH	69.6g
FAT	1.7g
OF WHICH SATURATES	0.5g
OF WHICH MONO-UNSATURATES	0.5g
OF WHICH POLYUNSATURATES	0.7g
FIBRE	2.5g
SODIUM	0.3g
SALT EQUIVALENT	0.1g

SUN'S SWEETCORN

Nutritional Information

Typical values (per 100g serving) drained

ENERGY	301KJ/71Kcal
PROTEIN	3.0g
CARBOHYDRATE	12.3g
OF WHICH SUGARS	6.5g
FAT	1.1g
OF WHICH SATURATES	trace
FIBRE	2.3g
SODIUM	trace
SALT EQUIVALENT	trace

3 Which food groups do you think contain the highest amounts of energy? Make a list.

Explain your choices.

4 For each of the energy types shown above, and on page 112, think of **one** other example of where you might find that type of energy. Put your answers in a table.

5 Can you think of some devices that use more than one form of energy?

Did You Know...?

The recommended daily intake of energy (in food) for boys aged 12–15 years is 11700 kJ and for girls of the same age is 9600 kJ.

FIGURE 2: What types of energy are shown in these photographs?

Changing energy

BIG IDEAS

You are learning to:
- Describe some useful energy changes
- Understand that not all the energy changes in a device are useful
- Apply the transformation model to some devices

Energy changers

All **machines** and devices work by changing energy from one form into another. These devices can be called **energy changers**. A torch works by changing chemical energy stored in the battery into light energy in the beam. Most energy changes involve more than one type of energy. For example, an electric fire changes electrical energy into heat and light. A television changes electrical energy into light and sound.

FIGURE 1: What is the starting energy and the end energy that makes this torch light up?

1 For each of the following devices, describe what the starting energy form is and what the end energy form is:
- **a** gas cooker
- **b** radio
- **c** hoover
- **d** washing machine
- **e** clockwork toy.

2 Draw a diagram to show the energy changes in:
- **a** a kettle
- **b** a computer.

Did You Know...?

Computers in the UK left on standby use 7% of the total electricity in the country! By turning things off you help save fuel and reduce your **carbon footprint**.

Non-useful changes

Televisions also produce heat, which is an unwanted or non-useful energy change. The heat does not vanish or get wasted or used up, but it is not a useful change. This happens in all devices.

3 Describe what you think happens to energy that is non-usefully changed by a device or a machine.

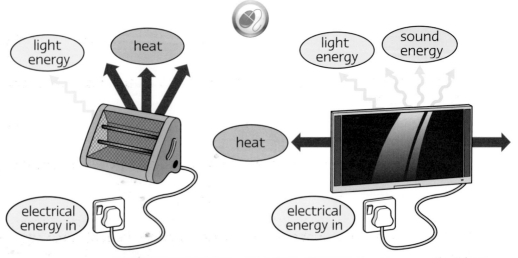

FIGURE 2: What are the non-useful energy changes in these two devices?

... appliances ... carbon footprint ... energy changers ...

Everyday energy changers

We often use electrical **appliances** at home and in industry because they can transfer energy easily, at the flick of a switch. This makes sure that an appliance only changes energy when it is needed to work.

Electrical energy is easily changed into heat, light, sound and movement by a range of devices. Electricity is also very useful because it is clean and non-polluting.

Your teacher will provide you with a range of things that change energy from one form into other forms. For each of the objects, decide: what the input energy is and what the output energy is.

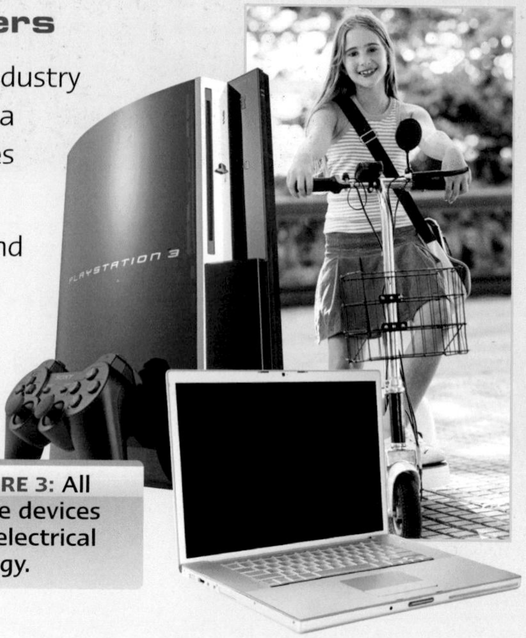

FIGURE 3: All these devices use electrical energy.

- Use a table like the one below to record your answers.
- Underline the useful output energy forms in each case.

Input form of energy	Energy changer	Output form(s) of energy
electrical	light bulb	light and heat
	solar panel	
	clockwork toy	
	immersion water heater	
	buzzer	
	stopclock	
	xylophone	
	candle	
	green plant	
	toy car on a ramp	
	reacting chemicals	

1 Write a brief report of your investigation. Include what you did and what you have found out.

2 What are the main advantages of using electricity as an initial form of energy in a range of devices?

3 If you repeated the investigation, what would you change to improve the quality of your results?

4 Why do you think that most energy changes produce heat at some stage in the process?

Tracking energy transfers

Drawing energy transfers

In the transfer model, the energy is located in one place. When something happens it is transferred to another place by a process.

Energy is transferred *from* the Sun *to* the leaf by light.

The weight lifter transfers energy *from* his muscles *to* the bar by moving his arms.

How do we track what happens to energy when it is transferred? It is useful to be able to draw a diagram to show how energy is transferred. This is called an **energy transfer diagram**.

FIGURE 1: These events need energy transfers to make them happen.

Input and output energy

Energy is transferred to a bulb by electricity and then from the bulb to the surroundings by the heat and light.

| mains | → | electricity in the wires | → | heat / light | → | surroundings |

FIGURE 2: How is energy transferred by a light bulb?

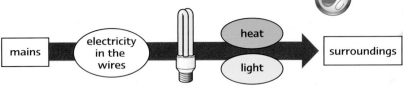

1 Write a sentence on the transfer of energy in:
   a an electrical drill   **b** a diesel car   **c** a television

2 Draw energy transfer diagrams for the following. On each one label the useful energy transfer.
   a a television   **b** a hoover   **c** a kettle

3 For each device in **Q2**, say what you think happens to the energy that is not usefully transferred. Why do you think this is?

Sankey diagrams

A **Sankey diagram** is used to show the *relative* amounts of energy transferred by a device. The width of each arrow shows how much energy is transferred. For example, the energy efficient light bulb below is provided with 100 J of energy as electricity and transfers 25 J as heat and 75 J as light. The widths of the output arrows show these proportions.

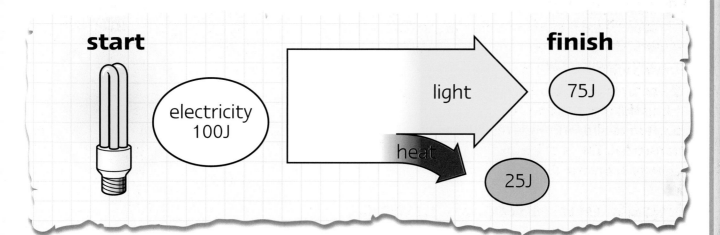

4 On squared paper, draw a Sankey diagram for each of the following energy transfer devices.
 a An electric drill that transfers 500 J of electricity into 100 J of heat, 100 J of sound, and 300 J of energy stored as movement.
 b A diesel car that transfers 5000 J from fuel into 2000 J of energy stored as movement, 1000 J of sound and 2000 J of heat.
 c A television that transfers 300 J of electricity into 200 J of heat, 50 J of light and 50 J of sound.

5 For each device in **Q4**, say what you think happens to the energy transferred as heat.

What are fuels?

You are learning to:
- Understand what a fuel is
- Identify some examples of fuels
- Investigate the products of combustion

What are fuels?

You may have heard the word '**fuel**' being talked about. A fuel is a source of energy. We use a lot of energy in our world and fuels provide most of it. We use fuels all the time. There are many different types of fuel. There are fuels that are solids, liquids and gases.

1 Make a table to show whether the fuel used by each thing in Figure 1 is a solid, liquid or a gas. Can you think of any other examples of fuels to add to your table?

2 a Write down **two** advantages of using petrol as a fuel for a car engine.
b What are **two** disadvantages of using petrol?

FIGURE 1: All these use fuels.

Common fuels

The fuels used most commonly are **coal**, **oil** and **natural gas**. In many parts of the world the only available fuel is wood. In very poor parts of the world people burn cow dung or peat. Often these people have to travel large distances to gather their fuels and they are careful about how they use them.

Coal, oil and natural gas contain large amounts of stored energy and release a lot of heat when they are burnt. Wood is not as good as it takes more of it to produce the same amount of energy. Peat is a poor fuel as it does not release much energy.

3 What are the **four** most commonly used fuels?

4 Compare oil with wood as a fuel.

Did You Know...?

In China, fuel was always in short supply so cooking food needed to be a quick process. This is why 'stir fry' cooking evolved in China.

... coal ... combustion ... controlled ... fuel ... low-grade fuel

Combustion

Burning fuels is a **combustion** reaction. It uses **oxygen** from the air. An equation can be used to show what happens during combustion:

fuel + oxygen → carbon dioxide + water (and heat)

Combustion reactions can be **controlled** or **uncontrolled**.

Unfortunately, burning fuels in any way creates **pollution**. Because most fuels contain impurities, they cause atmospheric pollution when they are burnt. Large amounts of the gases carbon dioxide, sulphur dioxide and nitrogen oxides are produced. These gases are released into the atmosphere where they can contribute to acid rain and global warming.

Burning coal produces large amounts of smoke and soot. When coal was a common industrial and household fuel it caused respiratory illnesses in people and lots of atmospheric pollution. In many parts of the developing world this is still a huge problem.

5   **a** What is a combustion reaction?
    b What are the products of combustion?

6   What problems does burning fuels cause?

7   What are the disadvantages of burning low-grade fuels?

8   Why do many countries still use low-grade fuels for heating, cooking and industry?

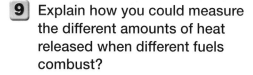

9   Explain how you could measure the different amounts of heat released when different fuels combust?

10   How could we measure the amount of heat energy that is produced when the candle burns. What difficulties need to be overcome?

FIGURE 2: Combustion reactions can cause great damage.

Exam Tip!

Fuels are not *forms* of energy (such as kinetic or heat or light energy) but they are *stores* of energy or energy *resources*.

Did You Know...?

It has been estimated that in Sub-Saharan Africa up to 80% of the population still relies on wood, animal dung, crop residues and grasses as a source of fuel. These are examples of **low-grade fuels**.

How Science Works

Investigating combustion – demonstration

The apparatus above is set up to show the products of combustion. When the candle burns, the products are drawn through the two test tubes. The cobalt chloride paper changes colour in the presence of water and the limewater changes colour in the presence of carbon dioxide.
What do you observe when the candle is lit?

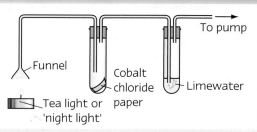

To pump

Funnel

Cobalt chloride paper

Limewater

Tea light or 'night light'

HSW

Energy release from fuels

BIG IDEAS

You are learning to:
- Recognise how energy from fuels is released
- Compare the amount of energy in different fuels
- Consider some of the alternatives to using fossil fuels as an energy source

Why we use certain fuels

FIGURE 1: Would you choose a liquid, solid or gas fuel to make this racing car go?

There are advantages (they come in liquid, gas and solid forms) and disadvantages (they cause pollution) of using fuels as our source of energy. The kind of fuel that we use depends on:

- what is available
- how much it costs
- what job we want it to do.

To release the energy that is stored in a fuel we need to **burn** it. The amount of energy that a fuel releases when it is burnt depends on:

- how much of the fuel is burnt
- the amount of energy that is stored in it.

1 What needs to be done to a fuel to release the energy stored in it?

2 What does the amount of energy released from a fuel depend on?

Fuels from plants

Recently different fuels have been developed using technology. Examples are bio-diesel, which is made from plant material and ethanol. Ethanol is a liquid fuel that is sometimes called alcohol. It is made from plants, especially sugar cane. In Brazil, where it is warm and wet, growing conditions are ideal for sugar cane. The country does not have large resources of fossil fuels to burn, so growing sugar cane to make ethanol is an attractive alternative. Ethanol is even used in cars instead of petrol. Many other parts of the world are now starting to grow crops used to make ethanol.

3 a State **two** advantages of using ethanol as a fuel.
   b State **two** disadvantages of using ethanol as a fuel.

4 Why have more countries started to grow sugar cane?

... bio-diesel ... burn

Finding the best fuel

The best fuel is the one that produces the most heat energy when it is burnt. Oil is the most-used fuel in the world today. Oil has a very high **energy density** and gives off more heat when it is burnt than other fuels.

FIGURE 2: Re-fuelling a passenger jet with aviation fuel made from crude oil.

You are going to compare the amount of energy contained in different fuels. You should also consider which is the cleanest burning fuel.

Your teacher will provide you with the apparatus that you may need for your investigation.

Method:

1   Write a plan for your investigation using the diagram on the right to help you. Begin your plan with a prediction of what you think will be the outcome. Remember to include safety notes. Ask your teacher to check your plan before you start.

2   Record your results in a suitable table and then draw a graph of your results.

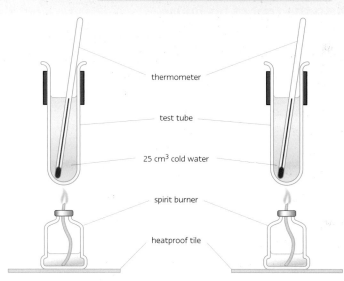

thermometer

test tube

25 cm³ cold water

spirit burner

heatproof tile

1   What were you trying to find out in your investigation?

2   How did you carry out your investigation? It may be useful to include a diagram of the apparatus you used.

3   What did you find out? Which was the best fuel?

4   Why was this fuel the best one?

5   What does the shape of your graph tell you about the amount of energy in each fuel?

6   Do you think your test was fair? Explain your answer.

7   How could you improve the design of your investigation to get more reliable results?

Energy efficient home in Devon village

Engineer Richard Bointon has taken his concerns for the environment into his own hands by building an 'eco-house' which will not only save energy but even sell it back to the National Grid! The electricity will be produced using solar panels on the roof of his house.

- The house is built from concrete blocks that have solid blocks of foam insulation on the outside. The foam keeps the concrete at the same temperature all year round and so saves Richard money on heating bills.

- The house also has a heat exchanger in the loft which takes warm, wet air from the bathroom and kitchen and uses it to heat up fresh air from outside. This is then blown into the bedrooms to warm them.

As cheap and plentiful energy becomes more scarce, it becomes more and more important to think of ways to make it last longer. Houses like Richard's take a lot of money to build but there are other things that we can all do.

One of the most important ways that we can save energy is by reducing the amount that we use to heat our homes. There are a number of ways that homes can be insulated to minimise the amount of heat that is lost by conduction, convection or radiation.

- Cavity walls in houses are often filled with foam to stop the air from moving through them in either direction. Modern wall insulation is light and compact. It has silvered surfaces to reflect heat back into the house.

FIGURE 1: Richard Bointon's eco-house.

- Lofts have layers of fibreglass in them. Fibreglass contains many small air pockets that prevent heat from moving; windows are double-glazed for the same reason. Some windows have a vacuum between the double-glazed panels to stop the heat being conducted through them.

It is hard to make old houses more energy efficient. For people living in older homes government grants are often available to help with the cost of insulation. Stricter planning laws mean that modern homes need to have energy saving features incorporated as part of their designs.

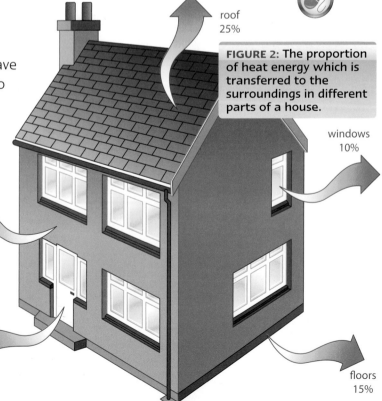

roof 25%

walls 35%

windows 10%

doors 15%

floors 15%

FIGURE 2: The proportion of heat energy which is transferred to the surroundings in different parts of a house.

Assess Yourself

1 Why is it important to prevent heat loss from homes?

2 Give **three** methods of insulating a house.

3 Suggest why older homes are more difficult to insulate than modern ones.

4 How is energy transferred from a house to the surroundings?

5 How has the transfer of energy been altered in the house in the photograph?

6 Explain why houses like this help to conserve fuels.

7 Why would a house like this cost more to build but less to run?

8 Explain how a house like this uses more of some kinds of resources and less of others.

9 Do you think that houses like this are a better use of resources? Explain why.

10 Why do you think the government provides grants to help people pay to have their homes insulated?

11 What impact does burning fossil fuels have on the environment?

Citizenship Activity

Find out what your local council is doing to help encourage people in your community to save energy. Make a plan of how you will find out before you begin.

ICT Activity

1 Use the internet to research some examples of modern energy efficient homes. What features have architects and designers used to help them with this process? Write a short report on your findings.

2 Go to the website http://www.think-energy.com/ThinkEnergy/11-14/activities and build your own energy efficient home!

Level Booster

8 You can explain the relationship between insulation and the rate of energy transfer and you can highlight the significance of these developments in the context of the debate about sustainable development. You can synthesise the key points to provide a succinct and balanced summary.

7 You can analyse how decisions about the design of such a house are made by including an understanding of energy transfer and the conservation of fuels, and how these contribute to sustainable development.

6 You can explain the choice of materials in the house by using the concept of energy transfer. You can justify a decision about the use of resources to construct such a house and compare this with the use of fuels.

5 You can explain how the nature of some materials reduces energy loss, and describe the implications of this for the amount of fuel used.

4 You can describe how the use of some materials reduces energy loss and how these can be applied to the design of a house. You can explain why it is important to conserve fuels.

Conductors and insulators

Electrical circuits

An **electric circuit** is a loop of wire that has its ends connected to an energy source such as a **cell** or **battery**.

Energy from a battery is carried around the circuit in the wire and is delivered to a device or **component** that is going to use it. When electricity flows through a complete circuit it produces an **electric current**.

In a circuit, one end of the wire is connected to the positive **terminal** of the battery; the other end of the wire is connected to the negative terminal. The wire is connected in this way so a current flows through it. A single battery is called a cell. Two or more cells connected together make a battery.

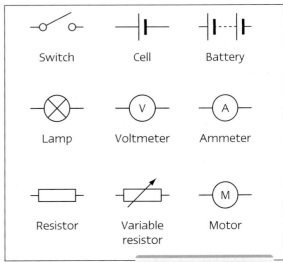

FIGURE 1: Common circuit symbols.

1 Why are circuit symbols used when drawing electric circuits?

2 What is the difference between a cell and a battery?

FIGURE 2: Two circuits showing how circuit symbols are used to represent actual components. Draw a circuit in your notebook that has three light bulbs in it.

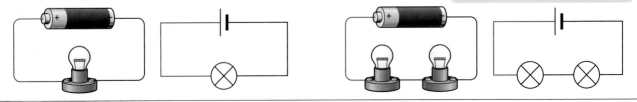

Measuring electric current

Electric **current** measures how much **electric charge** is flowing around a circuit. Current is given the letter '*I*' and is measured in Amps (symbol A). The more charge there is flowing in a circuit, the bigger the current. Current is measured using an ammeter.

Some types of ammeter have a pointer on a dial, but most have a digital readout.

Ammeters must be connected in series in a circuit so they can measure how much current passes through them.

FIGURE 3: An ammeter is used to measure how much current is flowing around a circuit. How much current is flowing in this circuit? (*Hint:* remember the correct unit!)

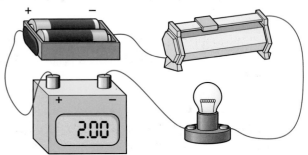

... battery ... cell ... component ... electric circuit ... electric current

Conducting electricity

In order for an electrical circuit to work, each of its components needs to allow an electric current to pass through it.

- A material that allows a current to pass through it is called an **electrical conductor**.
- A material that does not allow a current to pass through it is called an **electrical insulator**.

In this investigation you are going to find out how good different materials are at conducting current. Your teacher will provide you with the apparatus that you may need for your investigation.

Method:

1   Set up your circuit as shown in the diagram.

2   Test your bulb by touching the two crocodile clips together. The bulb should light strongly – if it doesn't your batteries are flat or the bulb is broken. Ask your teacher for help.

3   Copy the table below into your notebook to record your results.

ammeter

crocodile clip

material to be tested

Material tested	Bulb brightness	Ammeter reading	How good a conductor?
copper			
iron			
brass			
plastic			
carbon (graphite)			
glass			

4   Test each material in the table by connecting it between the crocodile clips as shown in the diagram. Write in your table how bright the bulb is, how much current flows and how good a conductor it is.

5   Test some other materials and objects around the room. You could add these to your table.

1   Write a short report to describe what you have found out. Make a list of all the good conductors in your investigation. Except for one material, what type of material are all the other good conductors in your list? Which good conductor in your list is the odd one out?

2   Explain why copper is usually used as the material to make wires from. What other materials could be used? What other properties of copper are important for their use in wires?

3   Explain the energy transfers that happen around the circuit. Why does the bulb light and not the conducting wire?

Current in circuits

BIG IDEAS

You are learning to:
- Recognise the differences between series and parallel circuits
- Understand what an electric current is and how it is measured
- Understand patterns in current flow

Series circuits

There are two main types of electric circuit, **series** and **parallel**.

In a series circuit:
- all the components are connected one after the other in a complete loop of conducting wire
- there is only one path that the **current** can take around the circuit
- the current passes through each component one after the other without branching off.

In a series circuit, if a bulb 'blows' or a component is disconnected, all the components stop working because a gap has been made in the circuit.

If more bulbs are connected in a series circuit, all the bulbs will be dimmer than before.

1 How are all the components in a series circuit connected?

2 What happens to the other components in a series circuit when a component is disconnected? Why is this?

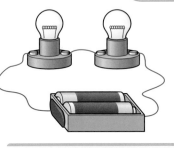
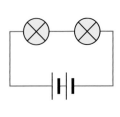

FIGURE 1: How can you tell that the components in this circuit are connected in series?

How Science Works

Christmas tree lights often don't work when they have been put away for a year.
This happens because the bulbs are fragile and may get broken when they are put away or got out again. What kind of circuit is used for them? Explain why one broken bulb prevents the rest from working.

Series circuits

In a series circuit:
- the current only has one path to take so it is always the same at any given point in the circuit
- the current does not get used up around the circuit – it flows through each component in turn
- the amount of current in the circuit depends on the number of cells and the number and nature of the components.

3 What is an electric current?

4 **a** How is an electric current measured?
b What is the unit of current?

5 State **three** facts about the current in a series circuit.

... branch ... current ... parallel

Parallel circuits

In a parallel circuit each component is connected separately in its own loop between the two terminals of a cell or battery.

A parallel circuit is rather like two separate series circuits connected to the same energy source. So the current has a choice of paths it can take.

The different components are connected on different wires. If you follow the circuit diagram from one side of the cell to the other, you can only pass through all the different components if you follow the **branches**.

In a parallel circuit, if a bulb 'blows' or a component is disconnected from one parallel wire, the components on different branches keep working. Unlike in a series circuit, the bulbs stay bright if more bulbs are added in parallel.

FIGURE 2: What happens to bulb **A** in this parallel circuit if bulb **B** 'blows'?

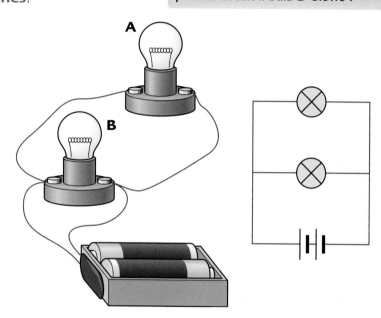

6 What is the difference between a series and a parallel circuit?

7 What happens in a parallel circuit when a component breaks? Explain your answer.

Current in parallel circuits

In a parallel circuit the current does not get used up, but it splits into different branches. The total circuit current is the sum of the separate currents in the individual branches. The current before the split is the same as the current after the split. How much current flows in each branch depends on the components in the branch. Each component has a separate **resistance** to the flow of current through it.

8 How is the total current in a parallel circuit worked out?

9 What does the amount of current flowing in each branch of a parallel circuit depend on?

10 Explain with reference to electric circuits what you think resistance means. What factors do you think would affect the resistance in a circuit? Explain why.

Energy in circuits

BIG IDEAS

You are learning to:
- Understand where the energy put into circuits comes from
- Explain what a voltmeter measures and how it is used
- Explain how voltage is shared by components in a circuit

Providing energy

We know that the current is not used up as it goes around a circuit, so where does the energy that is needed to light the bulb come from?

An electrical circuit allows the **transfer** of energy from a battery to the other components in the circuit. The chemicals in the battery are a store of energy. Chemical reactions in the battery release the energy to the circuit. When all the chemicals have reacted the battery will be 'flat'. When the circuit is complete energy from the battery pushes current around the circuit and transfers energy to each component, which then works, for example a bulb lights.

The energy or 'push' that a battery gives to a circuit is called the **voltage**. It is given the letter 'V' and is measured in **volts**.

Did You Know...?

Alessandro Volta (1745–1827) an Italian scientist, is credited with making the first electrical cell, and in 1881 the unit the 'volt' was named in his honour. He even has a crater on the Moon named after him – 'Volta Crater'!

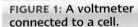
FIGURE 1: A voltmeter connected to a cell.

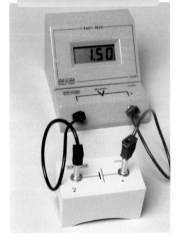

Measuring voltage

The amount of energy that a component is using is measured using a **voltmeter**.

A voltmeter must be connected in **parallel** with (across) a component to measure the energy difference in the current either side of the component.

The higher the voltage is the greater the amount of energy that can be transferred by a component.

How Science Works

Using a voltmeter
A voltmeter measures the energy transferred by a component. To do this it is connected in parallel with (across) the component to be tested as shown below.

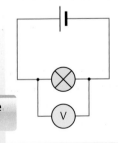
FIGURE 2: Connecting the voltmeter in parallel.

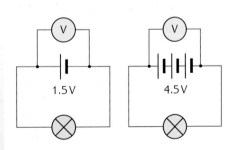

1.5 V   4.5 V

Measuring voltages across batteries.

... parallel ... parallel circuit ... potential difference... series circuit

In a **series circuit** the voltage provided by a battery is divided up by the components in the circuit. So how much voltage each single component gets depends on its resistance.

1 What does a voltmeter measure?

2 How is the voltage from a battery shared by the components in a series circuit?

The total voltage in a series circuit is the sum of the individual voltages across each component. This is shown by the equation:

$$V_1 = V_2 + V_3$$

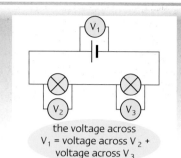

the voltage across
V_1 = voltage across V_2 +
voltage across V_3

Energy transfers in components

In a **parallel circuit**, the full voltage from a battery is available to all the components. This means that they can all work correctly at the same time.

So in a parallel circuit the stored energy in the battery is transferred more quickly and the battery runs out (becomes 'flat') sooner than if the components were connected in series.

Voltage is a measure of the difference in electrical energy between two parts of a circuit. Voltage is sometimes called the **potential difference (p.d.)**.

Potential difference measures the difference in the amount of energy a current is carrying either side of a component. The **voltage drop** across the component tells us how much energy the component is transferring.

3 Why can all the components in a parallel circuit work correctly at the same time?

4 Why must a voltmeter be connected in parallel?

5 How is the voltage from a battery shared by the components in a parallel circuit?

6 With reference to a series circuit, describe and explain as clearly as you can what the difference between an electric current and the potential difference is. Use ideas about energy in your answer. How are they related?

Watch Out!

Make sure you know the difference between current and voltage.
- Voltage is the energy that provides the 'push' to move a current around a circuit.
- Current is the movement of electric charge around a circuit.

The total voltage in a parallel circuit is the same as the voltage across a component in each branch. This is shown by the equation:

$$V_1 = V_2 = V_3$$

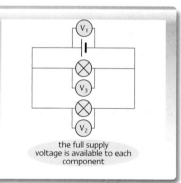

the full supply voltage is available to each component

Exam Tip!

Remember the rules:
- for voltage in series circuits use the equation:
$$V_1 = V_2 + V_3$$
- for voltage in parallel circuits use the equation:
$$V_1 = V_2 = V_3.$$
The voltage always drops across a component because energy is *transferred* by the component.

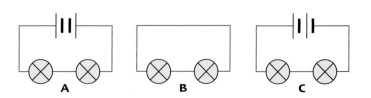

1 Tracy built three different circuits. Only one of them worked correctly.

Which one was it?

How do you know that this one would work?

2 Match up the device to the energy forms.

Kettle	Stored to kinetic, heat and sound
Electric light	Chemical to electrical to sound
Human body	Electrical to heat to kinetic and sound
Computer	Electrical to light and heat
MP3 player	Electrical to light, sound and heat

3 Machines work by transferring energy from one place to another. What are the energy transfers in each of the following cases?

   a A television   **b** An electric fire   **c** A motorcycle engine   **d** A match

4 Not all the energy that goes into a device is usefully transferred. Describe what happens to the rest of it

5 Complete the following sentences using the words from the list

        burnt   energy   fossil   light   non-renewable   oxygen

Fuels are stores of .... When they are .... they release this energy in the form of heat and .... They use .... from the air to burn. Most of our energy comes from .... fuels. Fossil fuels are .... energy sources.

6 Which of the following are non-renewable resources?

   a Wood and tides   **b** Oil and solar power

   c Coal and wind power   **d** Gas and oil

7 Draw circuit symbols for the following components

   ammeter   voltmeter   battery   bulb   resistor   two batteries in series.

8 **a** What is the difference between an electrical good conductor and an electrical insulator?

   b Which of the following materials are good conductors?

      air   aluminium   carbon   copper   cotton   glass   gold   iron   plastic   steel   wood

9 Complete the following sentences using the words from the list.

> ammeter   amps   conductor   current   current   higher   series

When electric charge moves through an electrical .... a .... flows. The .... is given the letter I for short. The current is measured in .... , using an .... which is connected in .... in the circuit. The .... the current the more electric charge flows.

10 Frank has just put some new light bulbs into his car. Lucy thinks that the bulbs are connected in series but Rakib disagrees and says that they will be connected in parallel. Who is right? Explain your answer.

11 Draw a circuit diagram to show how a light bulb can be lit from an electric cell. Include an ammeter in your diagram to measure the current, and a voltmeter to measure the voltage across the bulb

12 We can reduce some of the heat that is lost from our homes by using loft insulation.

   a Explain why loft insulation helps prevent heat loss from homes.

   b Modern loft insulation often has a silvered surface to make it more efficient

      Explain why this silvered surface helps.

   c Give **three** other ways to reduce heat loss from a house.

13 Explain what is meant by the term biofuel.

   a Give **two** advantages of using biofuels.

   b Name **two** biofuels.

   c Give **one** disadvantage of using biofuels.

14 Complete the following sentences using the words from the list.

> branches   current   current   current   highest   lowest   shared

In a parallel circuit the electric .... splits up into the separate .... of the circuit. The current is .... between the branches. The component with the .... resistance allows the greatest .... to flow. The component with the .... resistance has the smallest .... flowing through it.

15 Draw a scale Sankey diagram for a petrol tanker that uses 5000J of energy stored in fuel to produce 2000J of movement and 2000J of heat and 1000J of sound.

16 Compare and contrast the transfer and transform models of energy, giving reasons.

Topic Summary

Learning Checklist

☆ I can use words like kinetic, potential and chemical in my explanations — page 112

☆ I can give examples of how energy goes to waste — page 114

☆ I can describe the energy transfers in some devices — page 116

☆ I know that fuels release energy when they are burnt — page 118

☆ I can give some examples of how to save fuels — page 122

☆ I can build some simple circuits and draw them using circuit diagrams — page 124

☆ I can use the terms current, voltage and resistance in my explanations — page 126

☆ I know how to measure the current in a circuit — page 126

☆ I know the effect on the brightness of bulbs of connecting them in series — page 126

☆ I can build series circuits and draw them as circuit diagrams — page 126

☆ I know how current flows in series and parallel circuits — page 126

☆ I know that energy can be stored in various forms — page 112

☆ I can draw circuit diagrams of parallel circuits — page 126

☆ I know how to measure the voltage in a circuit — page 128

☆ I can link the number of cells in a circuit to energy transfers in circuits — page 128

☆ I can explain a variety of energy transfers — page 116

☆ I can use a model to show energy conservation (e.g. sankey diagram) — page 116

☆ I can describe the current in a parallel circuit — page 126

☆ I understand the effect on the current of connecting bulbs in parallel — page 126

☆ I know that the voltage change across part of a circuit is a measure of its energy transfer — page 128

☆ I can explain some of the problems associated with burning fossil fuels to generate electricity — page 118

☆ I can describe how the current in various parts of a parallel circuit is affected by the resistance of the components — page 126

☆ I can apply different models of voltage and energy changes to a circuit — page 128

☆ I can explain the advantages and disadvantages of using fossil fuels to generate electricity — page 118

☆ I can explain, using the idea of energy transfer, the effect of adding more components to a circuit — page 128

☆ I can explain the relationship between voltage and energy transfer — page 128

Topic Quiz

1 What are the energy transfers in:

   a a torch
   b a radio
   c a clockwork toy
   d a tree
   e a television

2 Give **five** forms of energy.

3 What is potential energy?

4 Give **three** ways in which we can insulate our homes.

5 What is a fuel?

6 Why is electricity such a useful form of energy?

7 What is the difference between a conductor and an insulator?

8 What is used to measure the current in a circuit? How is it connected?

9 What is used to measure the voltage in a circuit? How is it connected?

10 What is electrical resistance?

11 What does voltage measure?

12 What does current measure?

13 Give **three** differences between a series and a parallel circuit.

True or False?

If a statement is incorrect then rewrite it so it is correct.

1 Energy makes things happen.

2 Movement energy is also called kinetic energy.

3 Gravitational energy is the energy an object has due to its height.

4 Double glazing works by preventing conduction and radiation.

5 Fuels release stores of energy when they are burnt.

6 Conducting materials do not let an electric current flow through them.

7 Carbon is a poor conductor of electricity.

8 Putting more batteries into a circuit increases the current.

9 In a series circuit the current varies in different parts of the circuit.

10 A current will only flow in an incomplete circuit.

11 The current is measured with an ammeter.

12 A small voltage is needed to make a large current flow through a high resistance.

13 Most components have resistance.

14 Another term for voltage is potential difference.

Literacy Activity

Write an article about saving heat energy at home.

You should explain what methods you could use, why they work and why you need to do it.

You could choose to do this as:

- An article in a local newspaper
- For pupils in a primary school
- As a poem
- As a leaflet for local people
- As a poster for display in your school

The Land Speed Record

FIGURE 1: Thrust SSC on its record breaking run.

FIGURE 2: Thrust SSC

Ever since cars began to appear on the roads about 100 years ago, people have tried to go faster and faster. The fastest a car can go is called its top speed. As technology has improved cars have got quicker and quicker.

The land speed record (LSR) is held by the car that has travelled faster than any other vehicle at that point in time. The LSR is held by the vehicle which can travel at the highest speed through a measured distance. To make it a fair test the vehicle needs to travel both ways through the course. The distance that is used is a mile.

FIGURE 3: Donald Campbell's Bluebird which broke the LSR in 1964.

The average speed for the two 'runs' is then taken.

Many people have invested massive amounts of time, energy and money into their attempts to become the holder of the record. The challenge of becoming the fastest man on Earth has certainly inspired a select band of very brave men throughout the years. Many who succeeded in their quest were rewarded with fame, wealth and national honours. Many of those who failed were subjected to the most public and horrifying of deaths. As they have pushed the technology of the time to the limits there is always this risk to consider.

The current absolute (or unlimited) record is held by Thrust SSC, which is powered by a twin jet engine and which has achieved 763 mph (slightly under 1228 km/h) over one mile. In reaching this speed the car became the first land vehicle to break the sound barrier.

Two of the most famous holders of the record were the father and son Malcolm and Donald Campbell. Malcolm Campbell held the LSR on no fewer than nine separate occasions between 1924 and 1935. He also held the water speed record.

His son Donald set the world water speed record on seven occasions between 1955 and 1964 and broke the LSR in 1964. In doing so, he became the only person to hold both records at the same time. Between them, Donald Campbell and his father had set 11 speed records on water and ten on land.

BIG IDEAS

By the end of this unit you will know more about the effects that forces can have on objects. You will be able to measure the speed of an object and explain the effects of friction, air resistance and streamlining. You will be able to take measurements, understand their accuracy and when it is necessary to repeat readings.

FIGURE 4: Donald Campbell's Bluebird crashes at 300 mph at Coniston in 1967 killing him instantly.

FIGURE 5: Art Arfons with his car the 'Green Monster'.

Donald died at Coniston Water in the Lake District on 4 January 1967 when, while trying to break the 300 mph limit on water, he crashed. He had achieved a speed of 297 mph on the first leg, but on the return run the boat lifted out of the water after exceeding a speed of 300 mph, somersaulted and disintegrated on landing on the surface. Campbell died instantly.

In 1964, the record was pushed from 393 mph to 544 mph by the rivalry between the two Americans Craig Breedlove and Art Arfons. Both of the cars were powered by turbo jet engines.

The massive cost of developing vehicles to break the LSR has limited the number of recent attempts on the record. As speeds increase it becomes much more difficult for the driver of the vehicle to operate safely.

FIGURE 6: Craig Breedlove with the 'Spirit of America'.

What do you know?

1 What is meant by the top speed of a car?

2 What does the speed of a car depend on?

3 How can we tell if we are travelling fast?

4 What does the land speed record measure?

5 Why is it important that the car must travel both ways through the course?

6 Look at the photographs on the spread. What do you notice about the cars as they become more recent? Why do you think this has happened?

7 The LSR is measured over a mile. Why do you think that LSR attempts need much longer spaces than this?

8 Why do you think that there have not been any more recent attempts to break the existing record?

9 Why are LSR record attempts usually undertaken on dried out lake beds?

10 Why are parachutes used to help the car slow down at the end of a run?

Measuring the forces around you

BIG IDEAS

You are learning to:
- Describe what forces do to objects
- Recognise some examples of forces (in action) around you
- Explain the effect of force on a spring

What are forces?

Forces are all around us. We cannot see, touch or smell them but we do notice what they do. You produce forces all the time. They allow you to move, lift things up, jump, run, skateboard and do many more things.

Forces can be **pulls**, **pushes** or **turning** forces. When a force acts, it makes an object change its shape, speed or direction.

1 What are the **three** types of force?

2 What do forces do to an object?

Forces in action

When do we use forces? Here are some examples.

You use a pushing force to move a trolley around a supermarket, or press the keys on a computer keyboard or mobile phone.

You use a pulling force to shut a door. In a tug of war both teams pull the rope but in opposite directions.

FIGURE 1: Lance Armstrong, seven times winner of the Tour de France pushing his pedals.

A weight lifter pushes the weights upwards, but gravity pulls them down again.

A cyclist uses pushes and pulls to move the handlebars and make the pedals go round.

A footballer kicking the ball makes the direction the ball is travelling in change.

A car mechanic using a spanner applies a turning force.

3 Give some examples of pushing and pulling forces.

4 Why is a weight lifter only able to keep the weights up for a short time?

5 Using ideas about forces, explain why a large lorry needs a bigger engine than a car. Why does it take longer to stop?

FIGURE 2: Weight lifters use forces to lift.

elastic ... forces ... newton ... pulls

Making a force meter

It is useful to be able to measure the forces that are needed to get things to move. This allows scientists to compare their results and allows them to build machines to help us do jobs that we cannot do or cannot do very well.

The unit of force is the **newton** (N), which was named in honour of the English physicist Isaac Newton. The standard way of measuring forces is with a force meter. Most force meters use a stretching spring to measure the force. The greater the force that is applied to the spring, the more it **stretches**. The amount it stretches can then be measured. Springs are useful for this because they stretch evenly. They are said to be **elastic**. They stretch by the same amount each time the same weight is added. They return to their original shape when the force is absent.

You are going to build a force meter to measure some forces.

Set up your equipment as shown in the diagram.

Measure the length of the spring with no masses on it. This is your starting length.

Add weights to the spring and record how much it has stretched each time.
(Weight in N = mass in kg x 10)

Record your results in a table.

Draw a graph of your results using a set of axis like these:

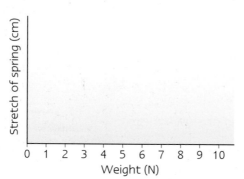

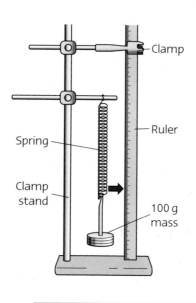

FIGURE 3: Making a force meter.

Questions

1 Describe and explain the pattern of your graph.

2 What happens to the length of a spring when you add weight to it?

Now you can use your graph to weigh things with your spring. If you hang other objects on the spring and measure how much it stretches, you can use the graph to find its weight.

3 How reliable are the results you obtained from your experiment? Do your results enable you to make accurate predictions about the weight of other objects? Explain your answer.

Different forces around you

BIG IDEAS

You are learning to:
- Recognise what forces do to objects
- Identify some examples of contact and non-contact forces

Types of forces

We have seen that there are many different types of forces and that they can all change the shape, speed or direction of motion of an object. The push and pull of forces is what keeps things where they are or starts them into motion. Whenever energy is being used then there are forces at work.

Forces can be further divided into two types called **contact** forces and **non-contact** forces. Many forces have to actually touch an object before they can affect it in any way. This type of force is called a contact force.

For example, you need to kick a ball to make it move so this is a contact force. Other types of contact force include:

Friction – the force that prevents objects moving or slows them down when they are already moving.

Air resistance – this is the force that you feel on your face when you are cycling fast. It is caused by friction between you and the air.

Upthrust – is produced by water pushing upwards on an object. It keeps things floating.

Surface tension – this helps raindrops keep their shape and allows some insects to move on the water surface.

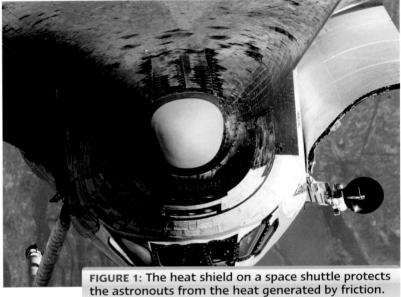

FIGURE 1: The heat shield on a space shuttle protects the astronouts from the heat generated by friction.

FIGURE 2: Upthrust.

How Science Works

Dragsters use parachutes to help them slow down. The parachutes work by increasing the air resistance or drag.

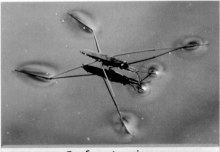

FIGURE 3: Surface tension.

1. What is the difference between a contact force and a non-contact force?

2. Give some examples of contact forces.

air resistance ... contact ... electric force ... friction ... gravity

Contact force rules

There are some rules that apply to all contact forces.

- The force exerted on each object only lasts for as long as the objects are in contact.
- The time that the objects are in contact is called the interaction of the forces.
- The forces only happen during the interaction.
- Once the objects are apart the forces no longer exist. The interaction of the forces has stopped.

It is important to remember that neither contact nor non-contact forces can be stored or put into any object. Forces rely on the interaction between two or more objects.

3 How long does the contact force on an object work for?

4 Summarise the rules about contact forces.

Non-contact forces

Some types of force can have an effect from a distance so they work without touching. These are called non-contact forces. Some examples of non-contact forces include:

Gravity – this is the force that pulls objects down to the centre of the planet and which gives them weight. Gravity is present between any two objects. Gravity can act over very large distances.

Magnetic force – the force produced by a magnet that affects magnetic materials such as iron and steel. Usually it only works over a short distance.

Electric force – from static electricity that can attract objects. This also tends to act over a short distance.

5 What is meant by a non-contact force?

6 Why do you think that gravity is stronger at long distances than the magnetic or electrical force?

7 What are common features of all the non-contact forces?

8 What is the main difference between gravity and the other two non-contact forces?

FIGURE 4: Gravity.

FIGURE 5: Magnetic force.

FIGURE 6: Electric force.

Balanced and unbalanced forces

Balanced and unbalanced forces

If the **forces** are equal in strength but opposite in direction then they are **balanced**. They do not make any difference to the shape, speed or the direction an object is moving in.

When the forces are not equal in strength or direction, or both, they are **unbalanced**. Unbalanced forces cause an object to change its shape, speed or direction.

Force diagrams

All forces are measured in **newtons**, which are given the letter N.

Forces always act in pairs, with one force acting in the opposite direction to the other force.

We can show the forces acting on an object by using arrows. In a **force diagram**, each force is shown by using a force arrow. The arrow shows:

- the size of the force (longer arrows for bigger forces)
- the direction in which the force is acting.

Normally the arrow is labelled with the name of the force and its size.

So, these arrows show the strength of the force in N and the direction in which the force is applied.

1 For each of the Figures 1 to 4, draw a force diagram.

FIGURE 1: An apple hanging on a tree.

FIGURE 2: A motor boat moving at a steady speed.

FIGURE 3: A space rocket taking off.

FIGURE 4: A plane braking after landing.

... *accelerate* ... *balanced* ... *decelerate* ... *force diagram*

Balanced forces and movement

When the forces acting on an object are balanced or there are no forces acting on an object, there are two possible effects.

If the object is not moving or is stationary then it will stay in the same place.

If the object is already moving then it will carry on moving in exactly the same way that it was moving before. Its speed and direction of movement remain unchanged.

2 What do balanced forces do to any object?

3 What happens to a stationary object when balanced forces act on it?

4 Draw a force diagram to show the forces acting on a car when it is parked on the roadside. Label the forces on your diagram.

FIGURE 5: A tennis ball floating in water is a good example of balanced forces in action.

Unbalanced forces and movement

When an unbalanced force acts on an object it often causes the object to change its **speed**.

This can make the object **accelerate** or slow down (**decelerate**). Which one depends on:

- the strength of the forces that are acting on it
- the direction the object is moving in.

Unbalanced forces can make an object change direction. When a footballer kicks a ball they make the direction that the ball is travelling in change as well as its speed.

5 Use a force diagram to show the forces acting on a car when it accelerates.

6 What is an unbalanced force? What do unbalanced forces do to any object?

7 Draw a series of force diagrams to show the forces that act on a space rocket from when it stands on the launch pad to when it is travelling at a constant speed through space.

FIGURE 6: The car is accelerating due to the force provided by the engine.

How Science Works

Tug of war – Using evidence

During a tug of war two teams pull a rope in opposite directions.

1 Using force diagrams show the forces acting on the rope in each of the following cases. For each one state which direction the rope will move in.

  a Team A and Team B pull with exactly the same force

  b Team B pull with a greater force

  c Team A pull with a greater force

  d Team B start stronger but then Team A apply a greater force

2 What happens when the forces are balanced?

3 What happens when the forces are unbalanced?

4 How could you carry out an experiment to test the actual forces that the two teams apply at any given point during the tug of war? What difficulties will you need to overcome?

Team A   **Team B**

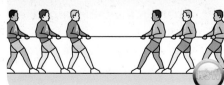

Speeding along

BIG IDEAS

You are learning to:
- State what is meant by speed
- Describe how speed is measured
- Calculate the speed of an object

What is speed?

When you travel on a journey it takes a certain amount of **time** to travel a **distance**. When you travel in a fast car you finish your journey more quickly than you would in a slow car.

The shorter the time taken to travel a given distance, the higher the **speed** is. The speed of any moving object tells us how long it takes to travel a certain distance. At high speed it takes less time to travel a certain distance than it does at low speed.

Comparing speeds

A car travelling at a speed of 30 miles per hour (mph) will travel a distance of 30 miles in one hour if its speed does not change. Road signs tell us what the maximum speed you are allowed to travel on certain roads is.

Some things move very fast and others move very slowly. Some examples of the speeds of different things are given in the table opposite. The speed of a galloping horse is 90 kilometres per hour. We write this as 90 km/h. The slanting line is short for 'per'. So the horse will travel 90 kilometres in one hour if it gallops at a **constant** speed. A constant speed is a speed that does not change during the journey.

1. What does speed measure?

2. What **two** things are needed to work out the speed we are travelling?

3. What do we mean when we talk about a constant speed?

4. How long would it take a bicycle travelling at a constant speed of 15 kilometres per hour to travel a distance of 45 kilometres? What have you assumed?

5. Why do you think there are different speed limits on different roads?

6. Where in the table opposite would you put:
   a) a skydiver in free fall (i.e. before the parachute opens)
   b) average speed of traffic in a town
   c) world speed record for a boat.

Did You Know...?

A motorised sofa, powered by a petrol engine, reached a top speed of 87 mph in 1998, making it the fastest piece of furniture ever.

Did You Know...?

Billy Baxter holds the world record for the fastest speed achieved on a motorcycle while riding blindfolded. He reached a speed of nearly 169 mph in 2003.

average speed ... centimetres ... constant ... distance

0.0036 km/h	Speed of a common snail	
6 km/h	A brisk walk	
36 km/h	Olympic sprinters (average speed over 100 metres)	
90 km/h	Peak speed of a galloping horse	
108 km/h	Typical speed of car (road), cheetah – fastest of all terrestrial animals, sailfish – fastest fish	
320 km/h	Typical speed of a high-speed train, a diving peregrine falcon – fastest bird	
350 km/h	Maximum speed of an Enzo Ferrari racing car	
1047.41 km/h	Top cruising speed of a Boeing 747-8	
3529 km/h	Official air speed record	
28 000 km/h	Space shuttle on re-entry	
300 000 km/s	Light waves	

Measuring speed

To work out the speed of any object you need to measure the distance that it has travelled and the time that it has taken to travel it. Distances are usually measured in **metres** (m), but they can also be measured in **centimetres** (cm) or **kilometres** (km).

100 cm = 1 m   1000 m = 1 km

average speed = distance/time

We measure the time taken in seconds (s), minutes (min) or hours (h). The speed is worked out by dividing the distance travelled by the time taken. We use this equation to help us calculate the speed.

We call this the **average speed** because the speed of any object rarely remains constant for a long period of time. The speed at which something moves varies on any journey. At some points it will be travelling faster than at other points. A car will slow down if it gets caught in a traffic jam and will speed up when it overtakes.

7 What is speed? How is it measured?

8 Why are average speeds often used for a journey?

9 A cheetah is the fastest land animal. It can cover a distance of 100 metres in four seconds when it is hunting. Calculate its speed in metres per second.

10 What factors will affect the top speed of a race car?

Speed Kills – So Kill Your Speed

Accidents on roads are almost as old as roads themselves, but as the number of road users has continued to increase so has the number of accidents. Because of the speed at which modern cars can travel these accidents are often fatal.

Research has shown that if a child is knocked over by a car at 40 mph there is an 80% chance that they will die. If the car is travelling at 30 mph there is an 80% chance that they will survive.

This research has led to the Government launching a nationwide campaign to get people to reduce their speeds, especially in towns.

This poster is part of the campaign.

FIGURE 1: Kill your speed.

But how do you get motorists to reduce speeds? One way is to use road humps and markings to reduce speeds. Another way is to use safety cameras (sometimes called speed cameras) to monitor the speed of motorists and fine motorists who go too fast.

Speed limits are set for the safety of all road users, and in built-up areas they are less than on open roads. As cars have become faster, more people are breaking the speed limits. This can be dangerous. In order to try to prevent people from breaking the speed limits safety cameras are placed at various points along roads.

They measure the speed at which a car is travelling and by photographing the car number plate can identify the owner of the car. Speed cameras are becoming a much more frequent sight on modern roads. They are designed to catch people who break the law by travelling too fast in their cars. Once caught, drivers are fined. If they are repeatedly caught they may be banned from driving.

As the amount of road traffic has increased in recent years so has the number of speed cameras. Speed cameras have become very successful and the number of people caught speeding has got much higher.

How do speed cameras work?

As cars have become more technically advanced so have cameras. Speed cameras today rarely rely on photographic film but instead use digital technology. There are three main types of speed cameras used in the UK. The first method used by Gatso and mobile cameras is to fire a laser or radar beam at the passing vehicle. The beam is then reflected from the car and returns to the speed camera equipment which uses a measurement of distance and time to calculate an exact speed. There are over 4000 fixed Gatso speed cameras currently in use by police forces and local authorities across the UK, accounting for 90% of all fixed speed cameras.

On some roads there are also time-and-distance cameras mounted on gantries over each lane: these take an image of the vehicle and the time of passing. Some distance on, the next camera computes the average speed at which the vehicle must have been travelling and triggers the fine if it is over the limit.

There are also mobile cameras set up by police at roadsides to record the speed of vehicles between two checkpoints.

There are a number of people who object to the increasing use of speed cameras on the roads.

FIGURE 2: A speed camera.

Assess Yourself

1   What is a fatal accident?

2   What is the chance of a pedestrian surviving an accident at 40 mph?

3   Why are speed limits set on the roads?

4   How is the speed of an object calculated?

5   Why are speed limits less in built up areas than they are on motorways?

6   Why do you think more people are breaking the speed limits today than 30 years ago?

7   What are the **three** types of forces? Illustrate each type by means of a simple force diagram.

8   What are the main differences between contact and non-contact forces? Give **three** examples of each type. What do contact and non-contact forces have in common?

9   What **three** things can happen when an unbalanced force interacts with an object?

10 Draw a force diagram to show a car moving along a road in each of the following situations. Label the forces correctly.
   a Moving at a steady speed.
   b Speeding up or accelerating.
   c Slowing down or decelerating.

ICT Activity

Use the Internet to research more about how speed cameras have developed over time.

Citizenship Activity

1   Undertake a survey of your local area to see how many speed cameras there are and what types they are. Do you think they have been effective in reducing accidents? What sort of information would you need to know to find this out?

2   How many road traffic accidents in your town are a result of people speeding?

3   There are other types of speed cameras used apart from the Gatso ones. Another common type is called the Truvelo camera. Prepare a short report to explain how this type of camera works and how it is different from the more common Gatso type.

Level Booster

8 You have demonstrated extensive knowledge and understanding and used it effectively in your explanation of the importance of these ideas in the context of speed limits.

7 You can explain some of the evidence used to support scientific ideas of forces and speed and you can give evidence of scientific progress helping to solve social problems.

6 Your answers show a good understanding of forces and speed, and you can use this to explain a range of unfamiliar situations. You can use models to explain the difference between contact and non-contact forces. You can describe some of the evidence to support the idea of forces acting on objects.

5 Your answers show a good understanding of forces and you can use this to explain balanced and unbalanced forces in a range of familiar situations. You can link the idea of speed to the forces applied to an object and you are able to describe the differences between contact and non-contact forces.

4 Your answers show a basic understanding of forces, which you can use to describe some processes and phenomena, and a basic grasp of some scientific terminology.

Measuring the speed

BIG IDEAS

You are learning to:
- Recognise the use of standard units of measurement
- Calculate the speed of some objects
- Evaluate the accuracy of an experiment

Measuring distance

Before we can start to work out the **speed** of an object, we need to measure the **time** that it takes and the **distance** that it has travelled. The more **accurately** we can measure these things the more reliable our results will be.

Distances can be measured in a number of different ways. Historically, measuring systems varied locally and were often defined by things such as the length of a stride or the size of the king's thumb. This made it very difficult for traders, merchants and scientists who all needed common units to work with.

Over time we have developed more ways to do this. We could pace out the distance, or use a tape measure. Nowadays we have very accurate GPS (Global Positioning System) which can pinpoint our position to within a **metre** anywhere on the planet. But what is a metre? To let them compare distances accurately scientists agreed to use the same measurement of distance. In the **metric system** the measure of distance is the metre. The metre is an example of a **standard unit** (SI) of measurement.

1 What is the standard (SI) unit of distance?

2 What advantages are there to agreeing to use the same system for measurements?

3 Why do you think traders and merchants needed to have common measurement systems?

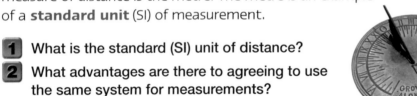

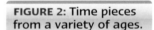
FIGURE 2: Time pieces from a variety of ages.

IMPROVED GREEK CLEPSYDRA

FIGURE 1: How could you measure how far away from each other the people in this photograph are?

Measuring time

The standard unit to measure time (*t*) is the **second**. Measuring time accurately is difficult. To measure time accurately needs good clocks.

A large variety of devices has been invented to measure time.

The most accurate timekeeping devices of the ancient world were the water clocks of ancient Egypt, which relied on dripping water. Sundials cast a shadow on a set of markings which were calibrated to the hour. The hourglass uses the flow of sand to measure time.

The most common devices in day-to-day life are clocks. As technology and engineering skills improved so clocks became more widespread and increasingly accurate.

4 What is the SI unit of time?

5 Why is it important to measure time accurately?

6 How have timekeeping methods improved?

accurate ... distance ... metre ... metric system

Measuring speed

You are going to measure the average speed of a number of different objects. If objects are travelling faster it is more difficult to calculate their speed accurately. The faster an object is travelling the more accurate the timing devices need to be. If the timing mechanism is not accurate enough then there will be more error in the results and they will be less reliable.

To let you measure time as accurately as possible you will be using some objects that are slower moving. You might be able to use a computer with light gates or a metre rule and a stopclock for taking your measurements.

Your teacher will provide you with some objects to time.

1   Try to predict the order of speed of the objects. Which will go fastest? To find out if you are correct you will need to measure out a distance and time how long it takes for the object to travel it. You can then work out the speed.

2   Decide on a distance to be measured. Should you use the same distance each time? What are you going to use to measure the distance?

3   Draw up a results table like the one below for recording your findings. What units are you going to use for distance?

Object	Distance travelled	Time taken (s)	Average speed

4   What will you use to measure the time taken?

5   For each object time how long it takes to travel the agreed distance and record your results. You can take more than one reading for each object if you want to.

6   Calculate the speed of each object and complete the table. What units will you use?

7   Draw a bar chart of your results. Why is a line graph not a suitable way to display your results?

Questions

1   Was your prediction correct?

2   Was your experiment a 'fair test'?

3   Describe how you could have improved your experiment to make it more accurate.

4   Explain why the speed of the object changes as it moves. Use ideas about forces and energy in your answers.

Friction

BIG IDEAS

You are learning to:
- Describe the effects of friction
- Recognise that friction is the force that opposes the movement of an object
- Recognise some examples of where friction is useful and where it is a problem

Friction and movement

Friction is a force that opposes motion. Friction is a contact force. Friction always acts in a direction **opposite** to the object's direction of **movement**.

To get an object to move, the force of friction needs to be overcome. To do this the force pushing or pulling the object needs to be greater than the force of friction which is preventing it from moving.

FIGURE 1: Friction between the slide and your body slows you down.

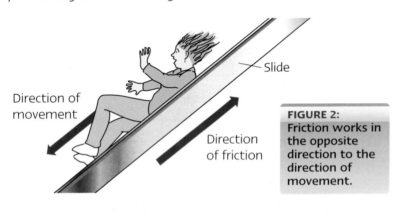

FIGURE 2: Friction works in the opposite direction to the direction of movement.

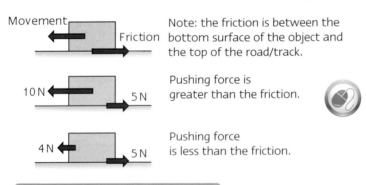

Note: the friction is between the bottom surface of the object and the top of the road/track.

Pushing force is greater than the friction.

Pushing force is less than the friction.

FIGURE 3: Friction and movement. Will the object move?

There are different forms of friction.

1. What is friction?

2. What does friction prevent?

3. How do we overcome the force of friction? What would happen if there was no friction between surfaces? Why?

Exam Tip!

Remember that friction will always act in the opposite direction to the direction of movement of the object. Friction acts to slow objects down or prevent them moving.

friction ... heat ... lubricate ... movement

Using friction

Friction produces **heat** and **sound**. If you rub your hands together the friction between the two surfaces makes your hands hot. In an engine the friction between the surfaces produces sound. There is less friction when there is a liquid (e.g. oil) between the two surfaces. There is more friction if the two surfaces are forced against each other, or if the objects are heavier.

Friction can be useful. It is friction between the tyres and the road which allows a racing car to stay on the track, but it also limits the speed that the car can reach.

When a vehicle brakes, the friction between the tyres and the road allows it to stop. On icy roads there is less friction so drivers need to be very careful.

To reduce friction, we can make surfaces as **smooth** as possible. Snowboarders and skiers use wax on the bottom of the snowboard or skis to make these surfaces smoother. This enables them to travel faster over the snow.

4 Give **two** ways to reduce the amount of friction between two surfaces.

5 Give **two** examples of ways in which friction is useful and **two** examples of ways in which it is a problem.

How Science Works

Look at the bicycle and see where you think friction might act. Then draw a table with two columns, one for where friction is useful and one for where it is a problem.

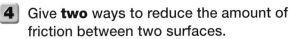

FIGURE 5: Friction helps tyres work.

FIGURE 4: Friction is lower on icy roads.

Explaining contact friction

Friction is a contact force. This means it only occurs when the surfaces are in contact with each other.

If we look at a smooth surface through a microscope we see that it actually has lots of small **rough** edges. It is these that cause the friction.

We can **lubricate** surfaces with oil or grease to help to reduce the friction between them. When we lubricate surfaces the lubricant gets into the gaps and makes the surfaces smoother. This allows them to slide over each other more easily and reduces the friction between them.

Car engines use oil to help lubricate the moving parts in the engine and make them work more efficiently and last longer.

6 What is a lubricant?

7 Explain how a lubricant works to reduce the friction between the moving parts in a car engine.

Air resistance

BIG IDEAS

You are learning to:
- Describe air resistance and its effects
- Explain what air resistance is using the idea of particles
- Apply the concept of air resistance to a skydiver's descent

Air resistance

When you travel down a hill on a bicycle your speed starts to increase. But as you go faster you also begin to feel the air on your face as you push through it. To cycle you have to push your way through the air. This pushing through the air sets up a force of friction called **air resistance**. Air resistance pushes against things that are moving. The faster you travel the more air resistance there is and the harder it is to go faster.

All vehicles have a top speed which depends on the amount of forward force that the engine can provide and the amount of air resistance that acts to slow it down. As a car gets faster the air resistance acting on it increases. The greater the air resistance the more the car is slowed down. This slows down the rate at which the car can accelerate and limits its top speed.

1 What is air resistance?

2 What things limit the top speed of a vehicle?

Explaining air resistance

Streamlining a vehicle helps to reduce air resistance. Increasing the surface area of an object increases air resistance.

Streamlining a car is a way of making it slip through the air more easily by reducing air resistance. Cars with narrow or wedge-shaped front ends and smooth, gentle curves slip through the air more easily than bulky vehicles such as large trucks with large, boxy, flat front ends.

Air is a gas and so the **particles** in it are spread far apart. When you are walking you are not travelling very quickly so you do not notice the air resistance very much. But as you go faster you **collide** more often with the particles in the air and these more frequent **collisions** start to slow you down. The more collisions that occur the greater the friction caused by the air particles and the slower you go.

3 How can we reduce the effects of air resistance on a vehicle?

4 Why do you notice air resistance more as you travel faster?

FIGURE 1: The streamlining of the car helps to reduce air resistance and the car has a higher top speed. The truck has a larger surface area than the car. This means air resistance is higher so it cannot go as fast.

Did You Know...?

Riding a specially modified £6000 bicycle, Fred Rompelberg, a Dutch cyclist, reached a speed of 166.944 mph in 1995, the fastest ever achieved on a bike. He was riding in the slipstream of a dragster which reduced the air resistance dramatically.

air resistance ... collide ... collision

Skydiving and terminal velocity

Even though the particles in the air are very tiny and very light, each collision causes a very small force on the moving object. Because there are millions of these collisions each second so millions of tiny forces add up to make a large overall force.

If the car is going faster, the air particles are encountered faster and more of them need to be pushed aside. The car will also hit the particles of the air harder. This increases the size of the tiny forces so the air resistance will increase.

Air resistance pushes against falling objects such as a person skydiving and this frictional force starts to slow them down. Skydivers do not need engines to make them move because their **weight** pulls them downwards.

FIGURE 2 A skydiver.

5 The following steps occur during a skydiver's descent. For each stage of the descent draw a force diagram to show the forces acting on the skydiver. The first one has been done for you (Figure 3).

1 When the skydiver leaves the plane she will accelerate downwards because her weight is greater than the air resistance (Figure 3).

2 As she accelerates the air resistance starts to increase because there are more air particles hitting her each second. Because her weight is still greater than the air resistance she continues to accelerate but the rate at which she accelerates starts to decrease.

3 After a while the air resistance has increased so much that it is the same as her weight. The forces acting on her are balanced so she cannot go any faster. She has reached a maximum speed or terminal velocity.

4 When she opens her parachute the air resistance suddenly increases. The forces acting on her are unbalanced and she slows down.

5 As she slows down the air resistance on the parachute gets less until it equals her weight. The forces are now balanced so she continues to fall at a steady speed. This is a new terminal velocity.

6 Explain using ideas about particles how air resistance slows down a moving vehicle.

7 What is meant by the term 'terminal velocity'?

8 Why does a parachute help to increase air resistance?

9 How could a skydiver increase his or her terminal velocity? Explain your answer.

Air resistance

Weight

FIGURE 3: The force diagram for step 1.

Streamlining and drag

BIG IDEAS

You are learning to:
- Describe what streamlining is and how it works
- Measure the speed of descent of different objects in fluids
- Use experimental data to understand the effects of streamlining

Streamlining

Streamlining vehicles reduces air resistance. This can increase their top speed and allow them to travel further on the same amount of fuel.

Wind tunnels enable engineers to study how the flow of air over an object affects both its speed and its stability.

If the shape of the object is smoothed out, many of the particles in the air are swept around it rather than colliding with it. This reduces the friction.

1 What are the advantages in streamlining an object?

2 Why are wind tunnels used to help car designers?

FIGURE 1: These vehicles have a streamlined shape to let them move more quickly and efficiently.

Moving through water

At a swimming pool it takes more energy to wade through the water than it does to walk along a road. This is because water is a much more **dense** material than air and it exerts a much higher resistance to your movement.

This type of frictional force is called **drag**. It is caused by friction from the water particles as the object tries to move through them.

Dolphins, sharks and porpoises have a streamlined shape, which reduces the friction, or drag from the water as they move through it. Their fins help them stay stable.

Boat builders use model boats and water tanks to design boats and **submarines** with as streamlined a shape as possible. The hull of a yacht is designed to cut through the water as efficiently as possible by reducing the drag force. Because frictional forces are much higher in water, objects cannot travel as fast as they can on land.

3 Why is friction higher in water than it is in the air?

4 Why do boats have a narrow, sharp bow?

Exam Tip!

Frictional forces in air can be called air resistance or drag but in water they are always called drag.

Did You Know...?

The Dead Sea in Israel has so much salt dissolved in it that you can easily float on it without a great deal of effort.

FIGURE 2: Can you see how the hull of this yacht cuts through the water?

dense ... drag

Investigating the effect of streamlining on the speed of descent

The slowing down of an object in water due to the resistance of the water particles is called drag. The greater the drag the slower the object will move. Streamlining an object reduces this drag force and allows it to travel more quickly.

You are going to investigate how the shape of an object and the density of the fluid will affect its speed through it.

You will be using three solutions in your investigation.

- Fresh water.
- Salt water – which is denser than fresh water because of the amount of salt in it.
- Wallpaper paste which is very dense.

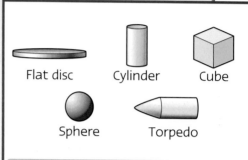

FIGURE 3: Possible shapes to investigate.

Your teacher will provide you with a range of equipment to use.

You will need to make a number of different shapes with some modelling material and measure their speed of descent through a set distance in each of the liquids.

1 Make at least **four** different shapes of model for your investigation. You should keep it a fair test by making sure that each shape has the same amount of material in it.

2 Predict which order you think they will finish in.

3 Measure out the distance that you will use. Try to make this as long as possible. A large measuring cylinder is ideal. You will need to use the same distance each time.

4 Release your shape and time how long it takes to get to the bottom. Record your results in a table. Repeat the experiment for each of the shapes.

5 If you have time try to get more than one reading for each shape.

6 Repeat the experiment using the salt water and then the wallpaper paste.

7 Use your results to calculate the speed for each object.

Write a brief report explaining what you did and within it try to answer the following questions.

Questions

1 Explain how you kept your experiment a fair test.

2 Which was the best shape? How do you know?

3 Was the finishing order the same for all three fluids?

4 How could you improve the design of your experiment?

5 What would you have to do to make the object more stable so it does not turn or twist while it descends?

6 How could you make the objects descend faster? Explain your answer.

7 How could you find out if any of the objects reached a terminal velocity during their descent?

1 Complete the sentences using words from the list.

force   larger   movement   newtons   scale   speed   spring   turning

A force can be a push, a pull or a _____ force. Forces make objects change their shape, _____ or direction of _____. The _____ the force is the more effect it has on the object. Forces are measured in _____, using a newton or _____ meter. Most newton meters rely on a _____ stretching. They then use a _____ to measure the amount of force.

2 Match up the force with the correct statement and effect.

Force	Statement	Effect
upthrust	upwards push from water	force opposing movement
gravity	force from air particles	slows objects down
air resistance	stops objects moving	used in hydraulics
friction	force acting on an area	makes things float
pressure	downwards force on the Earth	gives objects weight

3 Which statement is incorrect?

 A Unbalanced forces change an object's speed.

 B Unbalanced forces do not affect an object's shape.

 C Unbalanced forces change an object's direction.

4 Friction can be a useful force.

 a Give **two** examples of where friction can be useful.

 b Give **two** ways to reduce friction.

 c Why is it important to reduce friction in a car engine?

5 Robbie thinks that an object will only speed up if the forces acting on it are uneven. Rahala disagrees. She thinks that if an object is already moving, then an unbalanced force will make no difference to the speed.

 a Who is right?

 b Explain your answer.

6 Which statement is correct?

If the forces acting on a moving object are balanced, it continues to move at a steady speed in a straight line.

If the forces acting on a moving object are unbalanced, it continues to move at a steady speed in a straight line.

If the forces acting on a moving object are balanced, it continues to move at a steady speed but can change direction.

If the forces acting on a moving object are balanced, it continues to move at a steady speed but can change shape.

7 Race cars are often streamlined to enable them to travel at higher speeds. Describe how streamlining a vehicle reduces the air resistance acting on it.

8 Calculate the speed of the following:

   a A bicycle covering 250 metres in 30 seconds.

   b A skateboard covering 50 metres in 10 seconds.

   c A downhill skier covering 500 metres in 20 seconds.

   d A snail moving 20 centimetres in 3 minutes.

9 Which statement is correct?

Terminal velocity occurs when the forces of weight and air resistance are balanced.

Terminal velocity occurs when the forces of weight and air resistance are unbalanced.

Terminal velocity occurs when the weight is greater than the air resistance.

Terminal velocity occurs when the weight is less than the air resistance.

10 Why is the terminal velocity with a parachute open less than the terminal velocity before it was opened?

11 Why does air resistance increase with speed?

12 Why is the terminal velocity in water less than the terminal velocity in air?

Learning Checklist

☆ I can measure the size of a force and use the right units — page 136

☆ I can identify some different forces and describe how forces change movement — page 138

☆ I can explain the link between the speed of an object and the forces on it — page 140

☆ I can describe how forces change an object's shape, speed or direction — page 140

☆ I know how to measure distance and time and what units to use — page 142

☆ I know that friction is a force that opposes movement — page 148

☆ I know that upthrust pushes upwards and weight pulls downwards — page 150

☆ I can compare the speeds of different things and give some examples of streamlined objects — page 150

☆ I know what can increase friction, air resistance and water resistance — page 152

☆ I can identify the forces acting on an object and say which direction they are acting in — page 140

☆ I can describe situations where forces are balanced or unbalanced — page 140

☆ I know that if the forces on an object are unbalanced, it will either change shape or speed — page 140

☆ I can draw and use force diagrams with arrows to show the direction a force is acting in — page 140

☆ I can describe what speed means scientifically and use the correct units — page 142

☆ I can describe places where friction is useful and some ways of reducing it where it resists motion — page 148

☆ I know that air resistance is the force of friction of air on objects moving through it — page 150

☆ I can describe how streamlining reduces air and water resistance — page 150

☆ I know that if an object's speed changes then the forces acting on it must be unbalanced — page 140

☆ I know that if the forces on an object are balanced then it moves at a constant speed — page 140

☆ I can use the relationship between speed, distance and time — page 142

☆ I can describe how air and water resistance change with speed and begin to link these ideas to the particle model — page 150

☆ I know about the forces on falling objects — page 151

☆ I can use the particle model to explain scientifically why air and water resistance increase with speed — page 150

☆ I can explain how unbalanced forces cause an object to accelerate — page 140

☆ I can calculate speed, distance or time from the other two measurements and identify the correct units — page 142

☆ I can relate ideas and understanding about forces to situations in society, such as detecting drivers' breaking speed limits — page 144

☆ I can explain the relationship between the forces on a falling object — page 150

☆ I can explain, with reference to the particle model, what causes air and water resistance — page 150

Topic Quiz

1 In what **three** ways can we describe forces?

2 What **three** things do forces do to objects?

3 Name **three** contact forces.

4 Name **three** non-contact forces.

5 What are forces measured in?

6 How do we measure forces?

7 What happens to the speed of an object if an unbalanced force acts on it?

8 What does the term speed mean?

9 What **two** things are needed to work out the speed of an object?

10 How do we measure time? What units are used?

11 What is friction?

12 Why is friction greater in water than in air?

13 What is air resistance?

14 Give **two** examples of where friction is useful and two examples of where it is a problem.

15 Give **three** examples of streamlined objects.

16 Why is average speed often used to describe a journey?

True or False?

If a statement is incorrect then rewrite it so it is correct.

1 Forces only work from a distance.

2 When a football player kicks the ball, he only changes its speed.

3 Surface tension is only found in gases.

4 Contact forces only work for the short time the two objects are touching.

5 Forces are measured in kilograms.

6 Unbalanced forces do not affect the speed an object is moving at.

7 Ships float because their weight is greater than the upthrust from the water.

8 Speed measures the time taken for something to happen.

9 The units of speed are kilometres.

10 Friction is the force between two objects that allows them to move.

11 Terminal velocity is when an object reaches its maximum speed.

12 Terminal velocity occurs when the forces on the object are unbalanced.

13 Streamlining increases the drag force that acts on an object.

ICT

The distance that a car takes to come to a halt is called the stopping distance. The stopping distance can be split up into two parts or components, the thinking distance and the braking distance. The thinking distance is the distance that a car travels between the driver deciding to brake and the car actually starting to slow down. The braking distance is the distance that the car travels between the driver applying the brakes and the car actually stopping. There are a number of factors that may affect both of these. Use the internet or the library to research what some of these factors are.

Produce a written report or a presentation to show your findings.

FEEDING RELATIONSHIPS

Some animals feed directly on other animals.
These animals are called carnivores.
They are also called predators.
What features make them successful predators?

Some animals feed on plants.
These animals are called herbivores.
What features make them successful herbivores?

The Sun is the source of food for all organisms.
Firstly the sunlight is used by plants to obtain food.
Plants are green because they have a chemical that traps the sunlight.

Food chains show what animals eat. In simple terms, big animals eat smaller animals, smaller animals eat plants. In all habitats we can find out what an animal eats and what might eat it. Some animals will eat only one type of food e.g. koala bears will eat only eucalyptus leaves, others will eat one type of food but can change to a different food source if the first one runs out.

There are many places animals and plants can live

Old railway lines are quickly colonised by plants then animals. In cities, plants start to grow in the cracks on the pavements, animals such as pigeons, sparrows, foxes and rats feed off food that humans have thrown away.

Even the ice-cold conditions of the Arctic provide a home for penguins, seals and polar bears. Fish at the Arctic live in water that has a temperature of −10°C, they need a special type of 'anti-freeze' in their blood to stop them freezing.

The depths of the sea contain spectacular animals such as the anglerfish and giant squid. It seems if animals put their minds to it they can colonise nearly everywhere.

The cockroach is sometimes shown in science fiction as the 'beast' that survives nuclear fallout. This is not that far from the truth. It can survive ten times the level of radiation that we can. The cockroach is in fact very adaptable. It can eat glue, leather, books and it is reported to have eaten the plastic off the wires in television sets.

CLASSIFICATION AND FOOD WEBS

In November 1963, the island of Surtsey emerged in a fiery eruption from the Atlantic, it was 2.5 km² and rose to a height of 560 ft. The island has already been colonised by gulls, which have also brought moulds and bacteria. Seaweed and algae are now found there. Grasses, rushes and several flowering plants have been washed there. Over 20 species of plants and 20 species of animals, for example, mussels, butterflies and midges are now found on the island. It is a testament to the persistence of nature that some of these life forms came to Surtsey less than a year after it emerged.

BIG IDEAS

By the end of this unit you will know how living things are classified according to observable features. You will understand how some living things prey on others and how food webs indicate the flow of energy. You will be able to take evidence from different sources and produce explanations.

What do you know?

1 Write down the name of a plant in the pictures.

2 Write down the name of **one** herbivore in the pictures.

3 Write down the name of **two** carnivores in the pictures (secondary consumers).

4 Draw **two** food chains shown by the pictures.

5 What else could the lion eat?

6 What is the name of the process by which plants make food?

7 How are the buffalo adapted to feed on grass and escape the lions?

8 How is the rabbit adapted to escape from the fox?

9 How is the lion adapted to be a predator?

10 What might happen to the foxes if a disease wipes out the rabbits?

How do we classify?

BIG IDEAS

You are learning to:
- Use evidence to make decisions
- Explain the difference between vertebrates and invertebrates
- Recognise the difficulty in classifying some animals

What's in a name?

Using names for things helps other people know what you are talking about. However problems can arise! For example the viper and the adder are two different names used to label the same snake!

Now study the two photographs of bluebells in Figure 2. The plants shown are different but they have the same name.

1 Why is it better to have one name for a plant rather than two different ones?

2 Why is it difficult if two different animals have the same name.

FIGURE 1: A European viper or an adder? They are actually the same snake.

Classifying

Organisms can be sorted into the **plant** kingdom and the **animal** kingdom. The animal kingdom is then sorted into **groups** — 'with a backbone' and 'without a backbone'. This is called **classifying**. Each group is split into smaller groups. For example:

Animal kingdom

→ **Without a backbone** (**invertebrates**)

With a backbone (**vertebrates**)

Mammals, have hair | **Fish**, have wet scales | **Reptiles**, have dry, scaly skin | **Birds**, have feathers | **Amphibians**, live in water and on land

As the groups get smaller the features become more similar between the group members.

3 Study Figure 3 above and answer the following questions.
   a Do all animals have a backbone?
   b Do all mammals have a backbone?
   c Do primates have hair?

FIGURE 2: Both plants have the name bluebell, but they are different.

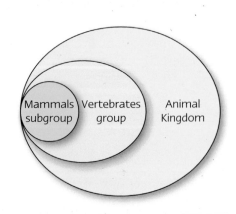

Mammals subgroup · Vertebrates group · Animal Kingdom

FIGURE 3: Classifying organisms into groups.

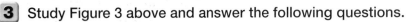

... amphibian ... animal ... bird ... classifying ... fish ... group ...

Vertebrates and invertebrates

Animals can be placed into two major groups:

- vertebrates — animals with a backbone
- invertebrates — animals without a backbone.

In general the invertebrates are simpler animals that have few complex organs. One success story of the invertebrate group is the insects. They are some of the most successful animals in the world. They can survive by eating paper, wood and oil. They are difficult to kill because they build up resistance to pesticides and reproduce quickly.

4 Why is an ostrich put into the vertebrate group?

5 Why is an ant put into the invertebrate group?

FIGURE 4: A rhinoceros beetle can carry up to 850 times its own weight! Why are insects so successful? Are they invertebrates or vertebrates?

Did You Know...?

In order to keep warm, warm-blooded animals need more energy than cold-blooded animals. This means they respire more and eat more regularly.

Vertebrate groups

There are five vertebrate **subgroups**. Each group has different features.

Fish – have gills; scales; fins; cold blooded

Reptiles – have dry, scaly skin; lay eggs with tough shells; cold blooded

Amphibians – have moist skin; live on water and land; breathe through their skin in water; cold blooded

Birds – have wings; beak; feathers; lay eggs with brittle shells; warm blooded

Mammals – have hair; give birth to live young; suckle their young; warm blooded

6 Give **two** differences between fish and reptiles.

7 Give **two** differences between mammals and birds.

What group do these belong to?

Figure 5 shows a whale and a shark. They both have fins, a tail and a streamlined shape. The shark has gills and the whale gives birth to live young and is warm blooded. The shark is therefore a fish and the whale is a mammal. It is sometimes necessary to look at several features before an animal can be placed in its correct subgroup.

FIGURE 5: One of these is a fish and one is a mammal. Which is which?

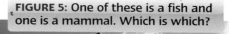

8 The photographs on the right show a duck-billed platypus and a turtle.
  a Explain, giving clear reasons, which subgroup of vertebrates each of the animals belongs to.
  b Explain, giving clear reasons, which other groups they could be put in.

The five kingdoms

BIG IDEAS

You are learning to:
- Recognise the wide range of organisms that exist
- Use evidence to make decisions
- Explain why changes have occurred in the way organisms are classified

Invertebrates

A **kingdom** is one of the major groups organisms are split into. The vertebrates and invertebrates are parts of the animal kingdom. The table shows the key **characteristics** of some of the invertebrate groups.

Cnidaria (Jellyfish)	Flatworms	True worms	Molluscs	Arthropods (all have an exoskeleton and jointed limbs.)			
				Insects	Arachnids	Crustacea	Myriapods
Jelly-like bodies. Tentacles. Hollow bodied.	Flattened. No segments to the body.	Cylindrical body. Segmented.	Soft body. Muscular foot. Many have shells.	6 legs. 3 body parts.	8 legs. 2 body parts.	Most have gills and antennae.	Many segments. At least one pair of legs on each segment.

1 Identify which of the groups the organisms below belong to, give reasons for your choice.

a

b

c

d

2 Give **one** other example of each major group.

... cell wall ... cellulose ... characteristics ... chlorophyll

The Plant Kingdom

Organisms were placed in the plant kingdom if they have a **cell wall** (made of **cellulose**), they can change light energy to chemical energy and contain **chlorophyll**.

Mosses	Ferns	Conifers	Flowering plants	Algae
Lack complex leaves, stems and roots.	Reproduce by spores.	Produce seeds in cones.	Seeds produced in flowers. Pollination by wind or insects.	Very simple organisms. No roots, stems or leaves.

3 Identify which groups the two plants in the pictures below belong to and give reasons for your choice.

a

b

4 Why is grass classified as a flowering plant?

5 Some scientists do not think algae should be classified as plants. Suggest why.

The Final Kingdoms

In the nineteenth century, scientists only used the plant and animal kingdoms for **classification**. It was found some organisms did not fit.

Fungi	Protista	Bacteria (Prokaryotes)
Cell wall not made of cellulose.	Mainly single celled.	Cell wall not made of cellulose.
Obtain energy from living or dead organisms.	Able to move.	No nucleus just genetic material.
Produce spores.	Some have cell walls.	Obtain energy from living or dead organisms.
No chlorophyll.	Some can transfer light energy to chemical energy.	No chlorophyll.

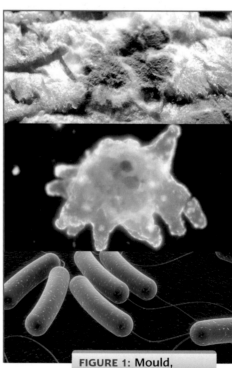

FIGURE 1: Mould, amoeba and bacteria.

6 Use the evidence to explain why:
a fungi **b** bacteria and **c** algae were originally classified as plants.
Explain why they created new groups to classify these organisms.
Which organism appears to be the simplest? Explain your choice.

Water for plants

BIG IDEAS

You are learning to:

- Explain how water is taken in by a plant
- Explain how water moves through a plant
- Use a model to explain how the cells are adapted to water movement

Water uptake

The water is taken into the plant through the **roots**. The roots grow downwards to find water.

The roots spread out underground to absorb the water and also to anchor the plant in the soil.

Did You Know...?

The tallest plants in the world are the Giant Redwoods in California. They are over 93 m in height and 9 m in diameter. The oldest one is 3200 years old.

1 Give **two** functions of roots.

2 Why might a plant send roots deeper down?

Stopping water loss

Once the water reaches the leaf, it is used for photosynthesis. The water is also used by the cells of a plant to cause them to swell and become rigid, this is like pumping air into a football to make it hard. To stop the water being lost, the leaf has a **waxy layer** around it. The water can still be lost through the **pores** in the leaf which let in carbon dioxide. The loss of water is called **transpiration**. The plant loses most water when it is hot, windy and dry. In desert conditions, the leaves of plants have a thick waxy layer, and are small or needle-like to adapt to the hot conditions.

3 Why do desert plants have a thicker wax layer?

4 In which conditions does the plant lose least water?

FIGURE 1: Why do plants have roots?

... large surface area ... pores ... root hair cells ... roots ... stem

Plant plumbing

Once the roots have taken in water, the water moves up a series of cells in the **stem**. We can see this in action using a piece of celery. If you place the bottom of it in red dye, and then section it, you will see red dots. These are stained cells. If you remove them, they are like red fibres.

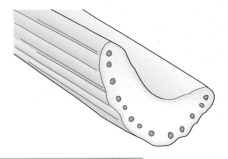

FIGURE 2: Cross section through a piece of celery

You can use lots of pieces of horizontally cut straw to represent the cells in the stem (xylem cells). Arrange them so that they form a pipeline, like the cells in the red fibre.

The cut straw is representing a cell. Remember your model plant cell (see page 11). Which parts of the cell have been removed? Why must the cell be hollow?

Importance of root hairs

The roots of the plant are adapted to take in water, they have **root hair cells** that have long extensions to penetrate between the soil particles and provide a **large surface area** to take up water. These hairs are very delicate and can be damaged when a plant is dug up.

5 Why does the root need root hairs for the uptake of water and minerals?

6 Plants need water to make them rigid. Why does a seedling wilt when it is transplanted from one pot to another? Why does covering seedlings with a plastic bag prevent them wilting?

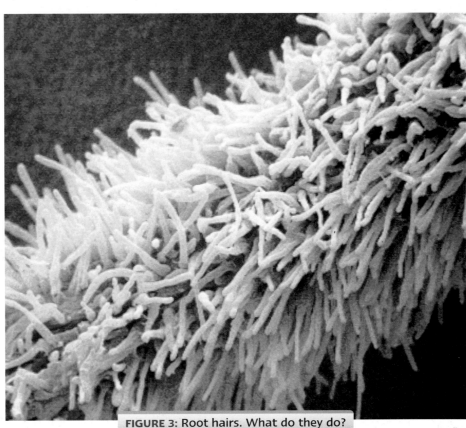

FIGURE 3: Root hairs. What do they do?

7 Draw a diagram to show the flow of water through a plant in the process of transpiration.

... transpiration ... waxy layer

Why do we need plants?

BIG IDEAS

You are learning to:
- Explain how plants make food by photosynthesis
- Describe how a leaf is adapted to photosynthesis
- Plan investigations from ideas generated

Nutrients needed

In the plant there are several organs that are important in the process of making food.

The roots are important for the uptake of water. The **leaves** trap light energy and take in carbon dioxide. The stem transports water to the leaves.

1 Describe what a leaf looks like.

2 How do leaves from different plants differ from each other?

FIGURE 1: Why do the branches of trees spread out?

Absorbing light

The leaf is adapted to trapping **light energy**. It has a large surface area to absorb light. It is thin so the light can reach the cells. It has a waxy layer to stop water loss.

3 Why is the leaf green?

4 The leaf has veins. Explain what they are for.

How Science Works

Scientists use a technique called chromatography, in which a leaf is ground up and the pigments are separated using a solvent. The pigments found are not just green but different shades of yellow as well.

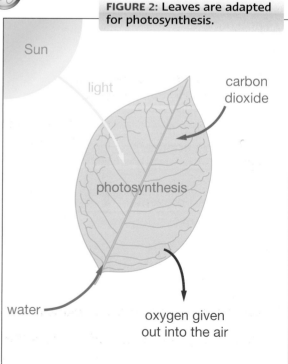

FIGURE 2: Leaves are adapted for photosynthesis.

Sun

light

carbon dioxide

photosynthesis

water

oxygen given out into the air

... chloroplasts ... leaves ... light energy

Photosynthesis

FIGURE 3: These trees are giving out oxygen. Why is this important to us?

The Amazon Rainforest is sometimes described as the 'lungs of the planet'. This is because the trees are giving out oxygen into the air.

The trapping of light energy by plants to make food and oxygen is called **photosynthesis**. In this process **chloroplasts** in the leaves trap light energy and use it to combine water with carbon dioxide to make a sugar (usually glucose).

$$\text{carbon dioxide } + \text{ water } \xrightarrow[\text{chlorophyll}]{\text{sunlight}} \text{ oxygen } + \text{ glucose}$$

The glucose is stored by the plant as starch. It is used for new growth or for respiration. The oxygen passes out of the leaf in the daytime.

Study the word equation for photosynthesis. How might you carry out tests to show a plant photosynthesising? Work with a partner to develop ideas in a poster.

5 Why does photosynthesis not occur at night?

6 Why do animals need plants?

Study Figure 3 carefully. Make sure you understand it shows the leaf is made of cells.

7 Explain how the palisade cells are adapted to trap light energy.

8 The pores allow gases to move in and out. Explain which gases move out in the daytime and which move in.

FIGURE 4: This is what a slice of leaf looks like under a microscope.

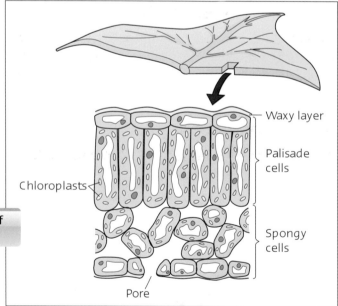

Waxy layer

Palisade cells

Chloroplasts

Spongy cells

Pore

9 What energy transfers take place in a leaf?

10 Describe the movement of particles through a green leaf.

Every year, the Royal Society for the Protection of Birds organises a Big Garden Bird Watch. They ask people to survey the numbers and species of birds in their gardens so they can keep track of what is happening to the bird populations. They have found that the numbers of birds from most bird species have been declining in gardens.

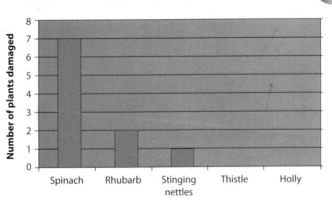

Mary is a keen gardener, and she also enjoys the wildlife that comes to her garden. She tries to encourage garden birds by looking after her plants organically (without using chemicals or slug pellets), by planting native species and by cutting the grass less often than her neighbours. This means there are more insects, slugs and snails for the birds to eat.

Mary does have a problem, though, with slugs and snails in her garden eating her plants. She notices that there are some plants that are often eaten, and some that the slugs and snails don't touch at all.

She plants a bed with ten plants each of spinach, rhubarb, nettle, thistle and holly and keeps a record of how many are damaged by the slugs and snails over a week. Here are her results.

Graph to show number of plants damaged by slugs or snails

(Bar graph: y-axis "Number of plants damaged" from 0 to 8; x-axis "Plant type")

Plant type	Number of plants damaged
Spinach	7
Rhubarb	2
Stinging nettles	1
Thistle	0
Holly	0

Here is some information about the plants.

Spinach: A dark green leafy vegetable that grows close to the ground.

Rhubarb: A plant with thick, brightly coloured stems, which are edible when cooked. The leaves contain oxalic acid, which can cause a sore mouth and acts as a laxative.

Stinging nettle: A herb which can be used to make soup, but which has toothed leaves and a stem with tiny stinging hairs.

These hairs are hollow tubes with walls of silica making them into tiny glass needles. The bulb at the base of each hair contains the stinging liquid, which includes formic acid. The tips of the hairs are very easily broken when touched. This leaves a sharp point, which can pierce the skin to deliver the sting.

Thistle: These plants have prickles all over their surface, including on the stem and the flat part of the leaf. Thistles can survive well in all sorts of environments.

Holly: Holly is an evergreen plant, which means that it has leaves even during the cold winter months. Each of the leaves has several sharp points. Holly berries are poisonous to humans, but can be eaten by birds and some animals.

Assess Yourself

1 Why do slugs and snails need to eat food?

2 Explain why slugs and snails prefer some of Mary's plants to others by referring to the features of the plants.

3 Explain the pattern in the data on the graph.

4 Write a food chain that names the producers, consumers, herbivores and carnivores in the garden.

5 Explain how energy is changed from light energy to energy in the thrush.

6 Suggest another plant that has 'self-defence' and explain how it deters herbivores from eating it.

7 Create a table of the plants mentioned in the text and summarise the features that each plant has to defend itself. Find out about other plants with self-defence and include them in the table.

8 Draw a food web of plants, insects and animals that are found in a garden. Show where the energy in the food web comes from. Choose one of the carnivores and describe what would happen to its population numbers if one of its prey items was removed.

9 There are some problems with Mary's data. Explain what these are and then explain what she could do to make sure her results were accurate and reliable.

10 Mary wants to encourage more thrushes to come to her garden to control the slugs and snails. Find out what habitat and food thrushes need and give Mary advice about how to manage her garden to attract more thrushes. Use what you know to explain why intensive farming methods threaten some bird species more than others.

ICT Activity

Using Microsoft PowerPoint, create a presentation to encourage people to manage their garden for wildlife.

Level Booster

8 You can transfer your knowledge of food webs to a wider context, for example by using what you know to suggest why intensive farming methods might create threats for some bird species more than others.

7 You can analyse, describe and explain what would happen to different organisms within a food web if one species was removed. You can use your knowledge of food webs to make suggestions about how to manage population numbers of a species.

6 You can link the process of photosynthesis to the energy flowing through a food chain. You can summarise information and research your own relevant information.

5 You can explain why the slugs and snails ate some plants more than others by relating the amount eaten to the characteristics of the plant. You can turn your food chain into a food web.

4 You can construct a simple food chain and use the keywords producer, consumer, herbivore and carnivore correctly.

Are leaves bigger in the shade?

BIG IDEAS

You are learning to:
- Understand how a plant responds to different conditions
- Present data in tables and graphs
- Interpret patterns and make conclusions from the data

The leaf

A **leaf** is an organ on a plant that traps light energy to make food. It has small pores on it that allow carbon dioxide to enter the leaf. These pores also let water out of the leaf.

1 Where does a plant get its water from?

2 Name **one** other factor that a plant needs to grow.

What affects leaf size?

The size of leaves is affected by the following:

- Amount of light. Bigger leaves trap more light energy to transfer to chemical energy in food than small leaves

- Amount of water. Big leaves lose more water than small leaves. If a plant loses too much water it starts to **wilt**

- Weight. Big leaves weigh more and need supporting.

FIGURE 1: Plants (such as the one shown on the left above) that live on the floor of rainforests need large leaves to be able to trap what little light reaches them to use to make their food. The giant redwood tree (above right) can grow to heights of 115 m. It has small, oval-shaped leaves as it is not shaded by other plants or trees.

Did You Know...?

The giant water lilies (*Victoria amazonia*) in Kew Gardens in London have a diameter of 2.5 m and weigh up to 45 kg. Each leaf is supported by strong rib-like structures on its underside. The leaf provides a large area for photosynthesis.

3 What happens to a plant if it loses too much water?

4 Predict whether a leaf grows bigger in the shade or the light and give reasons for your prediction.

5 The light energy is transferred to what form of chemical energy in the cell?

... adapt ... conditions ... distort ... leaf

Size of leaves

Plants **adapt** to living in shady **conditions** in different ways.

- The plant grows bigger (the leaves of dandelions growing in long grassland are bigger than the leaves of dandelions growing in short grassland).

- The plant makes more chlorophyll (the green pigment needed in photosynthesis to make food for the plant) in its leaves or grows larger leaves.

You are going to investigate the size of leaves on a plant grown in the light and on a plant of the same species grown in the shade.

Your teacher will provide you with the apparatus that you may need for your investigation.

FIGURE 2: These bluebells have many dark green leaves. Why?

Method:

1 Find several plants of the same species and of similar size growing in the light.

2 Remove 20 leaves from the same positions on the plants.

3 Measure the length and width to the nearest mm of each of the leaves.

4 Repeat **steps 2** and **3** for several plants of the same species and of similar size as in step **1** growing in the shade.

5 Put your results in a frequency table.

> **Exam Tip!**
>
> The larger the **sample size** the more **reliable** data are.
> A small sample size can **distort** data because unrepresentative results may be included.

Questions

1 Draw a frequency graph showing:
   a leaf width of plants growing in the shade and the light
   b leaf length of plants growing in the shade and the light.

2 How did you make the test fair?

3 Why did you take 20 leaves from the plants?

4 Is this a large enough sample?

5 What do your results show?

6 If your results show a pattern, suggest why this pattern occurs.

7 Plan an investigation to find out if dandelion leaves are longer in long grass or short grass.

What conditions do animals prefer?

BIG IDEAS

You are learning to:
- Plan an investigation into the conditions woodlice prefer to live in
- Present and interpret data

Where are woodlice found?

Woodlice are animals that are found in leaf litter. They are able to detect their environment with antennae, which are extensions at the front of the head.

1. In which areas are most woodlice found?

2. Suggest what conditions the woodlice might prefer.

3. Which **one** feature shows the woodlice are not insects?

FIGURE 1: A woodlouse. Can you see the antennae at the front of its head?

How Science Works

Design a simple investigation to explore the idea that there are more birds on the school playing field after lunch than before. Explain how you would collect reliable evidence.

What conditions do woodlice prefer?

Designing an experiment

You are going to use a **choice chamber** to find out if woodlice prefer dark or light conditions.

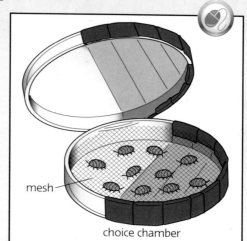

mesh

choice chamber

1 You will be provided with a choice chamber. One side of the chamber you will cover, both top and bottom, with black plastic.

2 You will then release at least six woodlice into the middle of the chamber and leave them for at least 1 minute to adjust to the conditions.

3 Then every 30 seconds for at least 2 minutes you will count how many woodlice are in the light.

You will make decisions about:

- How many woodlice to use
- How many sets of results to collect
- When a woodlouse is in the dark or light.

Record your decisions and explain why you made them. Carry out the investigation and answer the questions below.

1 Record your results in a table.

2 What conditions do your results show woodlice prefer?

3 Are there sufficient results to make a **conclusion**?

4 Explain why the woodlice prefer these conditions.

5 If you compare your results for the choice chamber experiment with those of other groups, would you expect them to be the same? Explain your answer.

Can woodlice detect 'colour'?

Design an experiment to see if woodlice prefer blue or red light. You will need to indicate how the data will be collected and recorded. You will also need to indicate how you can increase the reliability of the data.

How plants and animals survive

BIG IDEAS

You are learning to:
- Describe the basic needs for survival of animals
- Identify adaptations shown by animals and plants to their environment
- Explain what is meant by biodiversity

Animal survival

Animals are found in many different **environments**.

They have basic needs:

- source of food
- source of water
- an area of protection, from other animals or from extremes of the environment.

They need to live successfully in their environment so they **survive**.

1 Describe the conditions in Figure 1.

2 Name **one** animal other than the camel that lives in this environment.

3 What does the animal you have named feed on?

FIGURE 1: How does a camel survive in its environment?

Adapting to cold – or hot

FIGURE 2: The polar bear – adapted to cold and to hunt.

Success in surviving means that an animal must have special features that makes it suited to the conditions it lives in. This means it is **adapted**.

The polar bear is adapted to living in the cold and also to being a predator.

4 Which features adapt the polar bear for:
a the cold
b being a predator?

The cactus lives in the desert where it is very hot and there is a lack of water.

5 How is the cactus adapted to surviving in the desert?

FIGURE 3: Cacti are one of the few plants that can survive in the desert. How do they do it?

Did You Know...?

The cheetah is one of the fastest land animals. It can run at speeds up to 70 mph. In 2 seconds it can reach 45 mph. This makes it superbly adapted to catching its prey.

adapted ... biodiversity ... conserve

Many different habitats

The place an organism lives in an area is called its **habitat**. In woodland there are many different places for an organism to live. For example, different birds will feed on nuts, berries, caterpillars, insects and even mice. They will nest in different places. Some animals live underground, others in the trees, in leaf litter or under rocks. This means animals do not compete for the same sources of food or living space. Therefore the more varied the habitat, the more different types of plants and animals.

FIGURE 4: Badgers build dens under the ground in woodland.

6 What would happen to the numbers of birds if all the different birds ate the same things? Explain your answer.

7 What resources do plants in the woodland compete for?

FIGURE 5: Wildlife in a woodland.

Biodiversity

The number of different types of animals and plants in an area is called the **biodiversity**. An area with a high biodiversity, such as the rainforests, is rich in different plants and animals and would be an important area to **conserve**. Some areas are low in biodiversity but they contain very rare plants or animals. They also need to be conserved.

8 Why is the biodiversity greater in a rainforest than in open fields?

9 The Nature Conservancy uses a biodiversity measure to decide which areas should be conserved and which areas not. What are the advantages and disadvantages of doing this?

Food chains and webs

Food chains

Green plants are the start of all **food chains** because they can use light to make food. They are called **producers**.

Animals must feed on plants or on other animals, because they eat other organisms they are called **consumers**.

A simple food chain is shown: Grass ⟶ Grasshopper ⟶ Shrew ⟶ Owl

1 Name the producer.

2 Name a consumer.

3 What would happen to the animals if the shrew were poisoned?

> **Did You Know...?**
>
> The most ferocious carnivore for its size is the shrew. This animal only sleeps for about 4 hours a day and must eat regularly.

Food webs

Food chains do not show what really happens in nature. If the shrews died, the owls would eat something else. In a habitat there are many interlinked food chains that form a **food web**.

A simple food web is shown.

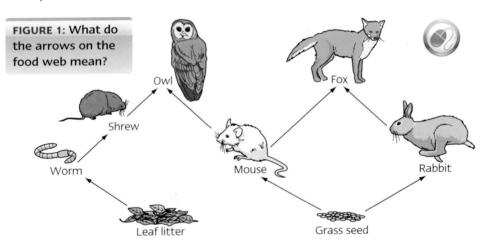

FIGURE 1: What do the arrows on the food web mean?

Owl
Shrew
Fox
Worm
Mouse
Rabbit
Leaf litter
Grass seed

FIGURE 2: Why is the fox at the to the food web?

4 Write down a food chain containing: **a three** links **b four** links.

5 If the mice died, give **one** thing that could happen to the rabbits in the food web.

6 Explain how the food web shows **energy** is transfered from the leaf litter to the owl.

... consumer ... energy ... food chains ... food web

Fragile webs

Some food webs are very complex and contain many different food chains. This makes the food webs less likely to be affected if one animal is wiped out, as there may be many other sources of food. Some of our habitats have simple food webs and are very fragile and easily affected by humans e.g. through pollution or hunting.

7 Why are some of our habitats fragile and easily damaged by humans?

Pyramid of numbers

In order to have enough food, an owl will catch several mice. This means there must be more mice than owls. The mice will also need to eat a lot of grass seed to survive.

If the number of plants and then the number of animals at each feeding level of a food chain are counted we will make a pyramid with the plants at the base. This is called the **pyramid of numbers**.

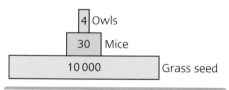

4	Owls
30	Mice
10 000	Grass seed

FIGURE 4: Pyramid of numbers for a woodland area.

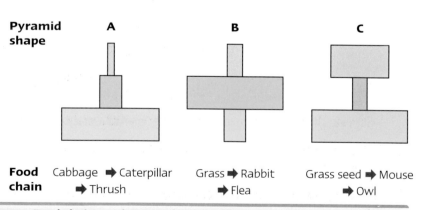

FIGURE 3: How is the owl adapted to catch its prey?

8 In the African savannah, why are there fewer lions than antelopes?

The number of producers is always along the base of the pyramid, then the herbivores (first consumer), secondary consumer and then the tertiary consumer.

A pyramid is not always formed, it depends on the size of the organisms.

9 For each food chain in Figure 5, match the pyramid of numbers formed and explain your reasoning.

Pyramid shape	A	B	C
Food chain	Cabbage ➡ Caterpillar ➡ Thrush	Grass ➡ Rabbit ➡ Flea	Grass seed ➡ Mouse ➡ Owl

FIGURE 5: Food chains and pyramids of numbers – can you match them up?

1 Leon was studying the organisms found in a pond. He looked up details of what the animals ate on the internet. He found out the following details.

Algae are green plants eaten by minnows.

Minnows are eaten by carp.

Carp are eaten by pike.

   a Construct a food chain from this information.

   b Which organism is the producer?

   c Name a consumer in this food chain.

   d What do the arrows show?

2 The picture shows an owl. Owls eat mice.

   a Give **two** ways the owl is adapted to catch mice.

   b Why does the owl catch several mice?

   c What could happen to the owls if the mice were killed by pesticides?

3 **a** Give **two** features the eagle has that put it in the bird group.

   b Give **one** similarity between birds and mammals that is not found in reptiles.

4 A plant needs to absorb light and water.

   a Why does a leaf have a waxy layer?

   b Why does a leaf have a large surface area?

   c Which cells in a root absorb most water?

5 A greenhouse is ideal for growing plants in.

   a i) Why are greenhouses better for growing plants in than a garden?

      ii) What are the problems of using a greenhouse?

   b A paraffin burner is used to heat greenhouses. It also produces carbon dioxide and water. What is the benefit to the plants of producing carbon dioxide?

   c What process transfers light energy to chemical energy?

6 The following pyramids of numbers were obtained from different environments.

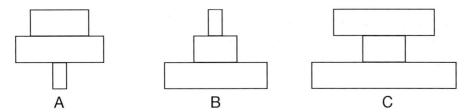

A   B   C

Which pyramid of numbers would be represented by the food chain:

oak tree → caterpillar → starling

Explain your answer.

7 A group of students are going to replant a flower bed in the school grounds to attract more butterflies. They want to investigate what kind of flowers they should grow.

a   What variables should they consider when selecting flowers to grow that might attract butterflies?

b   What criteria other than attracting butterflies should they consider?

c   Suggest a plan for their investigation.

d   How might they gather data on which to base a valid conclusion?

8 The Eden Project is designed to be a self-contained environment.

a   What does the environment in the domes have to provide for plants and animals?

b   Explain how this is a challenge in terms of populations and predator/prey relationships.

c   The level of carbon dioxide was measured for a whole day in summer in a greenhouse.

The graph shows the results.
i)   Describe and explain the variation in the level of carbon dioxide.
ii) Suggest how this might alter:
a) when winter arrives.
b) if more plants are introduced.

d   Comment on the assertion, 'Carbon dioxide threatens life.'

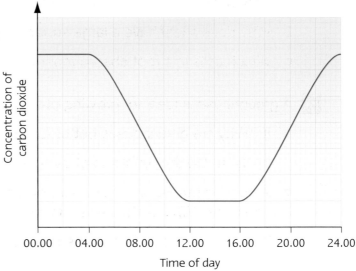

Topic Summary

Learning Checklist

☆ I know the five groups of vertebrates — page 160

☆ I know the conditions a plant needs for growth — page 164

☆ I know two conditions an animal needs to live — page 174

☆ I know that plants start a food chain — page 176

☆ I can identify the producer and consumer in a food chain — page 176

☆ I know the characteristics of mammals, fish, birds, reptiles and amphibians — page 160

☆ I can explain how a plant absorbs light and water — page 164

☆ I can name the adaptations a plant or animal have to survive — page 174

☆ I know the arrows in a food chain show the direction of energy transfer — page 176

☆ I can explain what happens to the organisms in a food web if one organism disappears — page 176

☆ I can classify unfamiliar organisms — page 162

☆ I know the gases used and produced in photosynthesis — page 166

☆ I can plan investigations into the conditions an animal prefers for survival — page 172

☆ I can construct a pyramid of numbers from given data — page 176

☆ I can explain how the cells of the stem are adapted to transport water — page 164

☆ I can write down the word equation for photosynthesis — page 166

☆ I can explain how a leaf cell is adapted to carry out photosynthesis — page 166

☆ I can explain why a leaf gives off oxygen in the day and carbon dioxide at night — page 166

☆ I can explain why pyramids of number are not always produced — page 176

☆ I can explain how energy is changed from light energy to energy in a carnivore — page 176

☆ I can explain why not all the energy reaches the carnivore — page 176

Topic Quiz

1 In a woodland the following food chain exists.

dead leaves ⟶ worm ⟶ shrew ⟶ owl

   a Which organism is the producer?

   b Which organism is the first consumer?

   c Which organism is a predator?

2 A lion is a predator that hunts antelope.

   a Give **two** ways in which the lion is adapted to hunt antelope.

   b Give **one** way in which the antelope is adapted to escape from the lion.

   c The antelope feeds on grass. What type of animal is it?

     Herbivore   Carnivore
     Omnivore   Predator

   d Construct a food chain for the three organisms.

3 Which organ in a plant is where photosynthesis occurs?

4 Which organ in a plant is used to take up water?

5 Give **two** reasons an owl is classified as a bird.

6 Why are worms classified as invertebrates?

7 What conditions need to be controlled in a greenhouse?

8 What **two** things does a paraffin burner provide in a normal greenhouse?

9 What happens to the sugar made in photosynthesis?

10 What is the word equation for photosynthesis?

Literacy Activity

Read the passage below, and then answer the questions.

Myxomatosis is a virus that infects rabbits. The symptoms are a watery discharge from the eyes and swelling of the eyelids and nose, followed by death in about two weeks. Myxomatosis has been used by humans to control rabbits in the wild. In 1952, an epidemic broke out that killed over 60 million rabbits (99% of the population). Biting or sucking insects such as the flea spread the disease. Burrowing rabbits were quickly infected. The killing of this many rabbits caused a serious fall in the number of buzzards. There was an increase in the number of foxes raiding chicken roosts. The grass on the downs grew quickly and many young shrubs grew into bushes. In 1952 it was made illegal to use infected animals as a means of spreading disease.

1 What does the rabbit eat?

2 Name **two** animals that eat the rabbit.

3 Why did the disease spread rapidly amongst burrowing rabbits?

4 Why did the population of buzzards drop?

5 Why was there an increase in bushes and shrubs?

6 Why was there an increase in foxes raiding chicken roosts?

7 Why do you think it is now illegal to use infected animals to spread disease to control pests?

Weather

FIGURE 1: Magic landscape.

magic

BIG IDEAS

By the end of this unit you will be able to describe the properties of rocks, and explain some of the ways that rocks are changed by physical processes. You will be able to communicate your ideas in various ways.

This is a very mysterious place. The earth pillars spread out all over the hillside, like a crowd of wizards in pointed hats. The pillars are constantly changing. They seem to collapse for no reason and then just vanish. It looks like magic. If you look more closely, the pointed structures all have something in common. All of them have a rock perched right on top, looking as though a giant put it there. The earth is strange too. It is a very rough mixture of soil and stones, with the sizes of the rocks varying enormously. Just how did these weird natural sculptures get here?

We now think we understand how the pillars form and why they disappear. The mixture of earth and rock is typical of a moraine, a heap of unsorted material dumped by a melting glacier. Whenever it rains in the mountains, the loose earth just washes away, unless there is a stone hat to protect it. As the soil is gradually removed by water, pillars start to form where the earth is protected by stones on top. The local Italians refer to them as Piramidi di Terra (earth pyramids). Eventually the rain weakens the pillars and the stone hat just slips off onto the ground below. The next rain will start to wash this pillar away, until no trace is left that it ever existed at all.

FIGURE 2: A closer look.

What do you know?

1. What is unusual about the landscape shown in the pictures?

2. How would you describe the appearance to someone who has never seen it?

3. What is the soil like in this area?

4. What is the origin of this special soil?

5. What is the importance of the stone at the top of each pillar?

6. What happens once a stone has fallen from the top?

7. What are moraines and what formed them?

8. What kind of weather is essential for the formation of earth pillars?

9. Why are you unlikely to find such landscape features in an arid environment?

10. How might you construct a model to show how these pillars form?

Looking at rocks

BIG IDEAS

You are learning to:
- Describe the appearance of rocks
- Sort rocks into different types
- Discuss the range of properties of rocks

Rock index

When you look closely at rocks they seem very different. Some rocks are packed with **crystals**. **Granite** is like this, we use it for kerbstones and for buildings. Rocks that are full of holes are from a volcano. **Lava** rocks are often full of gas bubbles. **Fossils** tell us about life in the distant past. We find fossils in rocks such as limestone. Different kinds of rock have their own special names.

FIGURE 1: Holiday on the rocks.

Rock type	Examples	Properties
Sedimentary	Limestone, sandstone, mudstone	Made of particles, in layers, often quite soft
Igneous	Granite, basalt lava	Crystalline, very hard
Metamorphic	Marble, slate	Changed by heat and pressure from earlier rocks, hard and shiny

1 What kind of rock is filled with gas bubbles?

2 Name **one** example of a changed rock and give the scientific name for rocks of this type.

FIGURE 2: Rock variations.

crystal ... fossil ... granite ... igneous

Rock types

There are three main types of rocks, as shown in the table on the previous page. Sedimentary rocks are the ones that contain fossils.

Look at some rock samples, examples of the three main rock types.

3 Examine each sample carefully and test the hardness with the point of an iron nail.

4 Look for signs of crystals, small regularly shaped particles usually with straight edges.

5 Check if the rock has layers of particles or can be split into layers.

6 Suggest the type of rock for each of the samples.

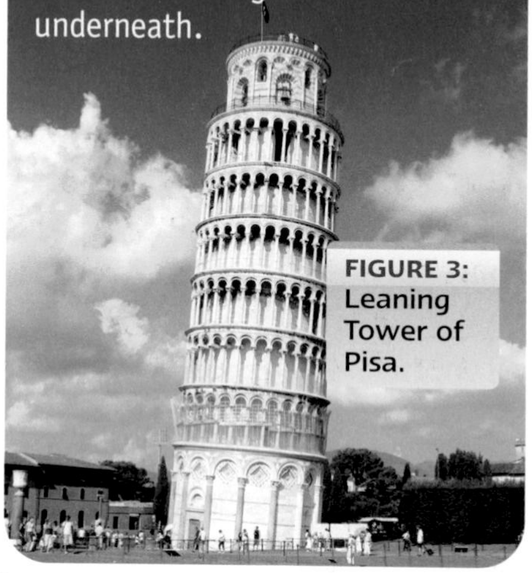

FIGURE 3: Leaning Tower of Pisa.

How Science Works

Use a hand lens or a magnifying glass to examine a sample of granite, an igneous rock. There are three different kinds of crystals in granite. The large ones are feldspar, the glassy ones are quartz and the shiny ones are mica.

1 Examine the sample closely using a lens.

2 Sketch what you can see.

3 Label each of the crystal types.

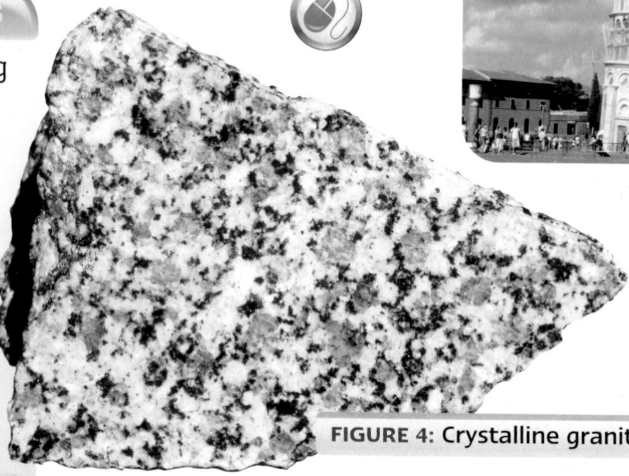

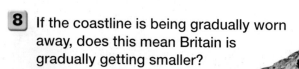

FIGURE 4: Crystalline granite.

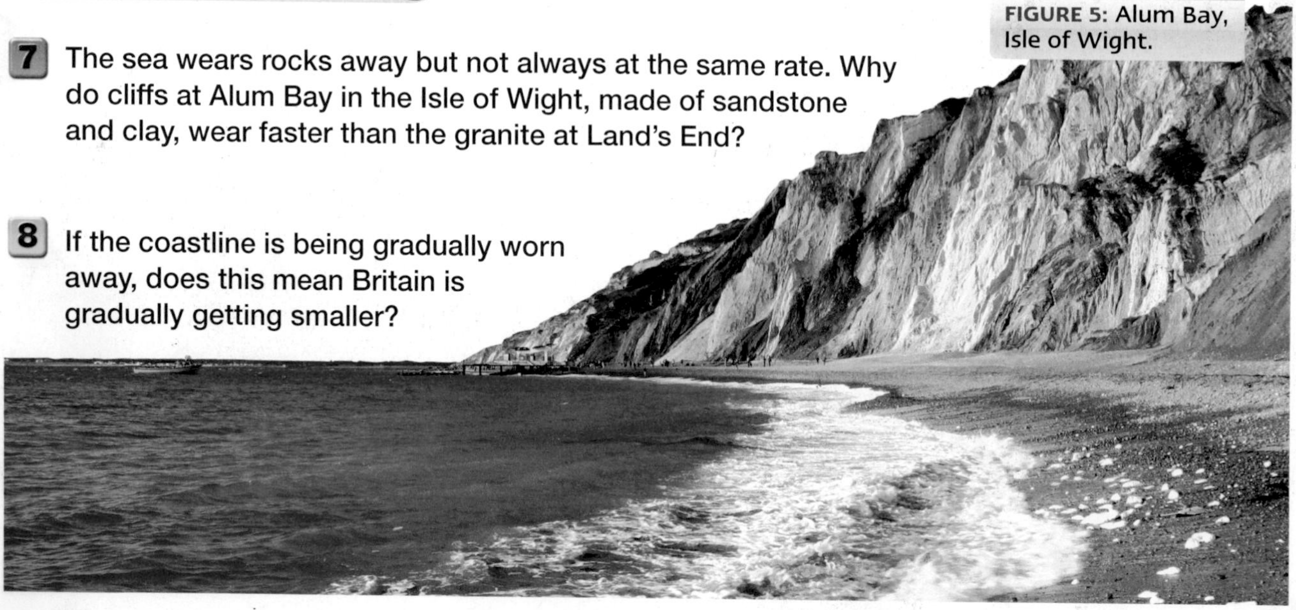

FIGURE 5: Alum Bay, Isle of Wight.

7 The sea wears rocks away but not always at the same rate. Why do cliffs at Alum Bay in the Isle of Wight, made of sandstone and clay, wear faster than the granite at Land's End?

8 If the coastline is being gradually worn away, does this mean Britain is gradually getting smaller?

... lava ... metamorphic ... sedimentary

BIG IDEAS

You are learning to:
- Draw conclusions from observations
- Investigate the properties of rocks
- Explain how these properties determine their uses

Using rocks

Damaged goods

St Paul's Cathedral was built after the Great Fire of London to replace an earlier building. It is made of limestone, **Portland stone** from southern England. This is one of the most popular building stones in Britain. It is easy to cut and to carve into shape and the stone lasts for hundreds of years. When St Paul's was new, all the stones were smoothed off. It is different now. You can see and feel the edges of curved shells raised above the surface of the stones. The shells are harder than the limestone and the rock has worn away around them.

Sandstones look like yellow and brown beach sand with all the sand **grains** stuck firmly together. They are held together by a natural cementing mineral. Old sandstone often shows a damaged surface to the rock. The rock cracks and splits and starts to turn back into loose sand again. One of the few rocks that seem to stay looking good is slate, used in thin sheets for roofing. Even slate roofing wears out eventually.

1. What kind of rock is Portland stone?

2. How can we tell if Portland stone has worn away?

3. Sandstones often contain traces of iron compounds. How does this explain their colours?

4. Suggest the various factors that an architect has to consider when selecting a building material. Why might there be more than one material that is suitable?

FIGURE 1: St Paul's Cathedral, London.

FIGURE 2: Sandstone.

grain ... Portland stone

Rock choices

Builders have to make sure that the rocks they choose are suitable. The rock must be strong, resist the weather and look good for many years. Compare samples of chalk, limestone and granite.

1 Describe each rock in terms of strength. Does it break easily?
2 Stand the samples in a tray of water. Do all of the rocks soak up water easily?
3 Decide which rock would be best for a kerbstone at the edge of a pavement. Explain your choice.
4 How could you use a balance to determine which of the three rocks was the most absorbent?

How Science Works

Sandstone challenge

Use small pieces of sandstone for this experiment.

1 Examine the sandstone using a lens and describe its appearance – colour, grains, banding.
2 Shake several pieces together inside a plastic box for 3 minutes.
3 Examine the pieces again and note any changes.
4 Explain why using sandstone for buildings might cause problems.

How Science Works

Slate science

The metamorphic rock called slate has been used for roofing for many years. Examine a roofing tile made of slate.

1 Test the hardness of the flat surface using an iron nail.
2 Examine the broken edge with a lens.
3 Describe what you can see. Try to explain why slates can break easily (cleave) in one direction only.

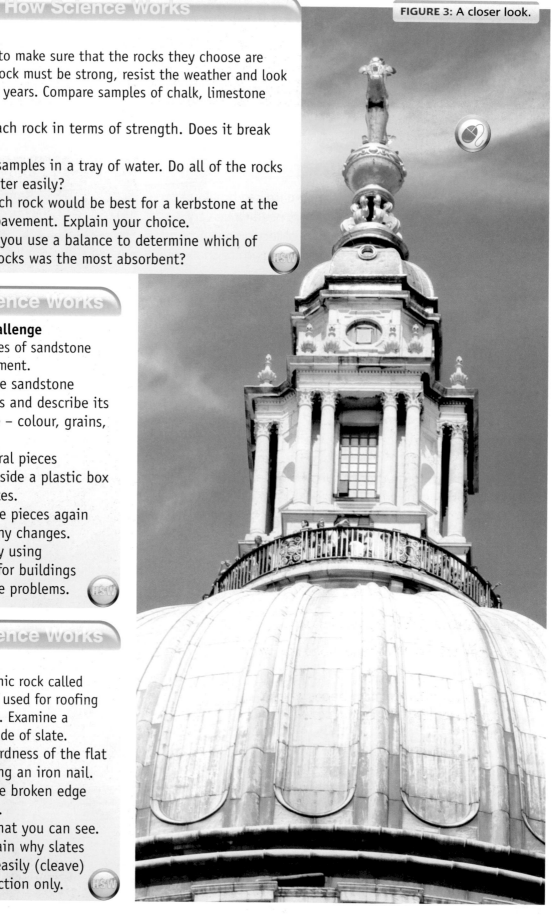

Mountain climbing

Rocks look very strong and hard. Rain and ice can break up rocks. We call this **weathering**. Climbers need to be very careful not to fall. Pieces of broken rock collect on the ground below. Some rocks wear away quickly, such as white chalk or mudstone.

1 What do we call it when rain or ice break up rocks?

2 Give **one** example of a rock that wears away quickly.

FIGURE 1: Dangerous sports.

Ice in action

Ice can cause major changes in rocks. Water has one special property when it freezes. The ice takes up more space than the water. Water **expands** as it freezes. When rainwater gets into cracks in rocks and then freezes at night, the force of the expanding ice is enough to break the rock. When the ice melts again, the rock fragments fall off. We call this freeze-thaw. This is what produces scree slopes in the mountains, piles of broken rock below a rock face.

Moving ice is even more destructive. **Glaciers** are slow moving rivers of ice that smooth out the landscape and carve glacial valleys.

How Science Works

Ice Power
1 Fill a bottle completely with water, leaving no air space at all.
2 Add strips of sticky tape to the outside for safety.
3 Leave the bottle in a freezer to let the water turn to ice.
4 Examine the result – it should look like the picture.
5 Describe what happens when water freezes and explain how a similar effect might break up rocks in nature.

FIGURE 2: Growing ice.

FIGURE 3: Glacier damage.

acidic... expands

Glaciers carry sand and broken rock along with them as they wear away the rocks below.

3 What is special about water as it freezes?

4 What is the effect of freeze-thaw in the mountains?

5 Why are glaciers like sandpaper?

FIGURE 4: A glacier.

Chemical and physical

Air naturally contains traces of the **acidic** gas carbon dioxide. When this gas dissolves in rainwater, the rain itself becomes weakly acidic. This is not the same as acid rain, produced by pollution. The naturally acidic rainwater can dissolve limestone, producing limestone pavements, caves and underground streams. The chemical change can be shown as:

FIGURE 5: Weathered limestone.

Calcium carbonate + acidic rain ⟶ solution of calcium hydrogen carbonate
When this water is boiled, you see crystals of calcium carbonate reappearing, known as limescale.

6 Why is the pH of rainwater naturally below 7?

7 Why do we find caves and stalactites only in limestone areas?

8 Why does limestone dissolve in rainwater?

9 What useful information about the past can you deduce from the scratches shown on glaciated rock?

How Science Works

Acid gas – demonstration
1 Boil some distilled water to get rid of any dissolved gases.
2 Test the pH of the water when it is cool.
3 Leave the water in a Petri dish exposed to the air for a few days. Test the pH again.
4 Try to explain any changes in pH in terms of carbon dioxide gas in the air.

Pebble and powder science

BIG IDEAS

You are learning to:
- Understand that sand has a history
- Explain that patterns in particles contain clues
- Investigate transportation of sand by wind

Wearing away the rocks

When rocks are weathered, only the hardest materials are left. The commonest one is sand which forms the famous sand dunes in the desert. Sand grains are blown by the wind into amazing moving patterns. Sand dunes are always on the move. Whole cities have been buried in the moving sand, only to be rediscovered by archaeologists.

Desert sand grains are rounded. As the grains bump into each other, all the sharp corners are worn away. If you look closely at a sandstone building and the grains are rounded, then the sandstone was formed in a desert.

1 What causes sand dunes to grow and to move?

2 What shape are desert sand grains?

FIGURE 1: Sand mountains.

Get sorted

Water can also sort particles according to their sizes.

As you walk along this famous beach, you notice something odd. The grains at one end are small but, the further you walk, the larger the pebbles become. Local people can tell exactly where they are with their eyes shut, just from the size of the stones. Both wind and water can sort particles into patterns that may be preserved in the rocks.

3 What do we mean by a shingle beach?

4 What is unusual about the beach shown in the picture?

5 What would happen if you dropped a large pebble at the wrong end of the beach?

6 Most beaches worldwide are made of sand, the mineral called quartz. What does this tell us about the resistance of this mineral to weathering?

FIGURE 2: Magic in the shingle.

Flying sand grains

High winds in the desert can wear rocks into weird shapes. The lighter the sand grains, the easier for winds to lift them into the air. The investigation looks at how the wind can sort sand by the size of its grains.

Method:

1   Fix the fan or hair dryer to blow a stream of air along the bench.

2   Place a long strip of white paper on the bench, starting at the fan.

3   Mark distance lines every 10 cm on the paper.

4   Switch on the fan and very slowly drizzle dry sand just in front of the fan. Continue until 200 g of sand has been added.

5   Take a sample from each 10 cm section using sticky tape. Press the tape on to the sand and then fix it on white card, in the correct order.

6   Using a magnifying glass, check how the size of the grains varies with their distance from the fan.

Did You Know...?

Sand dunes contain waves of sand, one layer flowing over the next. When the sand is preserved as a sandstone, you can see these wavy patterns in the rock.

FIGURE 3: Wind power.

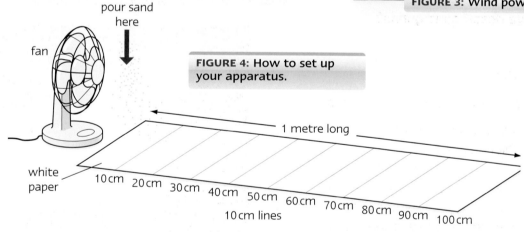

FIGURE 4: How to set up your apparatus.

pour sand here

fan

white paper

10 cm 20 cm 30 cm 40 cm 50 cm 60 cm 70 cm 80 cm 90 cm 100 cm

10 cm lines

1 metre long

Questions

1   Why is it important to use dry sand?

2   What pattern did you find in your results?

3   What would be the effect of increasing the power of the fan, as in a desert storm?

4   Explain how these ideas might apply to pebbles in a stream.

Rapid weathering

BIG IDEAS

You are learning to:
- Understand how surface area and particle size are related
- Use models to help understand weathering

Sweet science

If you want to eat a sweet very quickly, you must crush it into little bits first. The smaller pieces dissolve more easily and then disappear. Weathering of rocks is similar. Large blocks of rock are broken down by the weather. The smaller pieces have a bigger **surface area** when you add all of them together. Each time a piece breaks, new surfaces are made on each side of the split. Smaller pieces of rock are easier to move, as in streams. Then they wear away even more which is why pebbles are usually smooth or rounded.

FIGURE 1: Sweet enough.

1 How does weathering change the size of rocks?

2 Why are weathered rocks easier to move?

Speeding it up

If you want to watch the effects of weathering on rocks you need patience. It might take hundreds of years. To speed things up we can use a model of a rock to see what happens. Plaster of Paris is used to set bone fractures and also to make toy models. By pouring liquid plaster into a mould you can make a complicated shape, such as a cartoon character. The problem with plaster is that it is very **brittle**, it breaks easily. Plaster is easy to form into any shape required and sets solid quickly. This makes it a good choice for a model to represent a rock.

3 Why is it often difficult to study how rocks weather?

4 What is meant by a brittle material?

5 Why is plaster a suitable material for a model rock?

6 Explain how wave action on a beach that is covered in loose rocks might cause cliffs to be eroded.

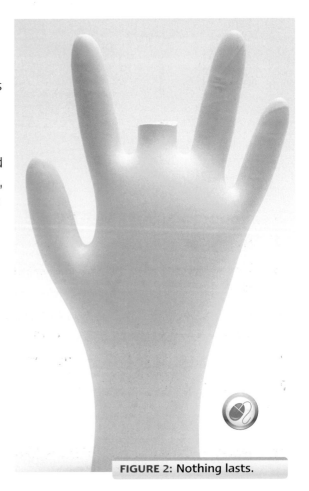

FIGURE 2: Nothing lasts.

brittle ...

Weathering with cubes

Method

1 Choose five of the plaster cubes and write a reference letter on each face of each cube, six for each. This will let you find them again later.

2 Weigh each of the marked cubes using a balance.

3 Replace all the cubes in the bottle and seal it.

4 Shake the bottle 10 times to represent rock particles being moved around in a stream.

5 Tip the cubes out on to a tray.

6 Examine the marked cubes and note any changes. Weigh them again.

7 Repeat steps 5 and 6 for a total of 20, 50 and 100 shakes.

8 Record your results in a copy of the following table.

FIGURE 3: Pieces of rock.

Cube letter	Mass at start	After 10 shakes	20	50	100	Changes seen
A						
B						
C						
D						
E						

Questions

1 What happened to the shape of the cubes?

2 How did the mass change?

3 What new material did you see in the bottle after shaking?

4 What is the likely final shape of the cubes if you continue shaking?

Did You Know...?

In deserts, the winds can sandblast rocks and wear them away. The wind blows the sand grains against the rocks and smoothes them. The same idea is used to clean old buildings. Sand is blasted under pressure to remove dirt from the stone of the building. The buildings often look new again.

5 How good a way is this of investigating what happens to pebbles at the seashore?

... surface area

Five hundred years after the sculptor Michelangelo carved the now world-famous statue of David out of a single block of marble, the piece of art was put through the most careful and painstaking cleaning in its history.

The naked statue, which is over five metres high, is now housed under a glass dome in the Galleria dell'Accademia in Florence, Italy. It was brought into the gallery towards the end of the nineteenth century to protect it from the weather. Franca Falletti, director of the gallery said "Unless this had been done, city pollution would have caused terrible damage to the marble". After the original was taken into the Galleria dell'Accademia in 1873, it was given a brief soak in acid that made it even more vulnerable to dirt, dust and the breath of more than a million visitors a year.

If you walk to the gallery in Florence, you can see dirt and acid erosion on the outside of Florence's Cathedral, the Duomo, which was thoroughly cleaned only ten years ago. The city of Florence houses some of the world's most famous art and sculpture, and new methods to preserve these priceless pieces of art are always being developed.

David was cleaned by an art restorer, Cinzia Parnigoni, using distilled water and cotton swabs. The cleaning cost £270 000, and took over 18 months to complete.

"I mixed together cellulose, clay and distilled water to make a sort of cream, and then wrapped it in Japanese rice paper before applying it. The paper let through the water, but stopped the paste coming into contact with the surface," said Ms. Parnigoni. The

hardest part was David's curly hair. "That was where it was most difficult to get the pack in."

Apart from doing battle with the weather and pollution, the statue has survived a more recent attack in the gallery. Ten years ago, a man hit the foot of the statue with a hammer. Some good did come out of the attack, however, as the gallery was able to send a sample of the marble away for analysis. This analysis was carried out before the restoration, to help to plan the method of cleaning.

The Michelangelo masterpiece attracts more than 1.2 million people every year.

Here is some information about different types of stone to help you with your answers.

Type of Stone	Examples	Properties
Sedimentary	Sandstone, limestone, chalk, shale	Formed in layers React with acid in rain and erode Quite soft and can be crumbly
Igneous	Granite, basalt	Formed from interlocking crystals Some types (e.g. granite) are very hard, others softer
Metamorphic	Marble, slate	Formed from other rocks under great pressure and/or high temperatures Hard Some types (for example marble) are expensive

Assess Yourself

1 What is pollution?

2 Give some examples of the sort of pollution that might be found in a city.

3 Explain how pollution can cause acid rain.

4 Why would city pollution have 'caused terrible damage to the marble'?

5 Why do you think the statue was cleaned with acid in 1873?

6 How would you have known whether a chemical reaction was taking place between the acid and the marble?

7 Use the table to explain whether marble was a good choice of material for a statue.

8 Write a word equation for the chemical reaction that would damage the statue.

9 The article says the statue is at risk from people breathing. Explain in detail why this is.

10 Suggest what sort of experiments you would carry out on the chips of the marble from the statue to help you to decide the best method of cleaning.

ICT Activity

Go online to find pictures of Michelangelo's David statue before and after the restoration. Create a quiz in PowerPoint to test whether your classmates can tell the difference.

Level Booster

8 You can also explore how Science changes over time as new evidence comes to light, and use this to explain why the cleaning treatment today is so different from in 1873.

7 You can summarise what you have learnt about rocks so it can be easily understood and make a justified decision about which rock would be best for the statue to be carved from. You can use a chemical equation to describe one type of chemical reaction that would cause the stone to look worn. You can explain how weathering and erosion fit into the rock cycle.

6 You can explain why rocks erode and describe how weather conditions would affect different types of rocks. You can draw a conclusion about what type of rock would be best for carving an important statue and justify why you made the decision.

5 You can describe the properties of metamorphic, igneous and sedimentary rocks and link this to which would be the most suitable to make a statue from. You can explain what erosion is and how it might affect how long a statue lasts.

4 You can explain what pollution is and how it can cause acid rain.

Transporting rocks

BIG IDEAS

You are learning to:
- Describe how rocks move around
- Explain how sediment can be moved
- Use a model to investigate a situation

Fast and slow

Rivers are like conveyor belts. The load moved by a river includes sand, mud, stones and anything that has dissolved in the river water. Rainwater can dissolve materials from the rocks and the soil. This is how the dissolved materials get into the river water. Other materials including sand and stones are just carried along by the moving water.

It is not very surprising that fast flowing rivers can carry more material than sluggish ones. Calculations show that doubling the speed of a river increases the load it can carry by 60 times. In the mountains it is obvious that the torrents of water are moving much larger stones than would be possible with a slow moving stream.

If you stir sand in a bucket of water, it goes into **suspension**, the moving water holds it up. Stop stirring and the water slows down. The sand just settles out. Rivers are the same. When a river reaches the sea it slows down and drops its load. This is how **deltas** form. The banks of sand and mud will turn into new rocks, sandstone and mudstone.

FIGURE 1: Moving load.

1. Which part of a river's load is it impossible to see?

2. What do we mean by the phrase 'in suspension'?

3. Why does a river move more material after heavy rain?

FIGURE 2: Water on the move.

Testing a model river

You can use a model of a river to understand how sand and other sediment can be moved.

1   Set up a gently sloping 2 metre length of plastic guttering as your model river.

2   Spread out a mixture of mud, sand and hard pebbles near the top of the slope.

3   Place a very large clear plastic box at the lower end to catch the flowing water. This box is like the sea.

4   Use a hose to spray water at the start of the model river.

FIGURE 3: The end of the river.

Questions

1   Describe what happens in the model river and any differences in the ways the separate materials behave.

2   Which of the original rocks must have been harder, the one that became pebbles or the one that became mud?

3   Describe what happens as the material collects in the box.

4   Water in a river usually slows down as it reaches the sea. Use the picture and the model to explain why sandbanks and pebble beds form near the mouths of rivers.

5   Explain why rivers often deposit mud far out to sea.

Rocks and heat

BIG IDEAS

You are learning to:
- Explain how heat changes things
- Describe how to recognise changes to rocks
- Use evidence to examine explanations

New rocks for old

Rocks can be **baked**. The heat changes the rock, just like in cooking. We call these **metamorphic** rocks, which means changed rocks.

Metamorphism is caused by a combination of heat and pressure. Metamorphism can be local, around a volcano, or it can affect a whole region. The original rocks are altered producing new colours, bands and crystals. Metamorphic rocks are usually very hard.

Metamorphic rocks are often better at resisting weathering. There are some exceptions where metamorphism destroys the strength of the original rock.

FIGURE 1: Oven chemistry.

1 Which metamorphic rock can you see on roofs?

2 Why are you unlikely to find fossils in marble?

3 Name **two** kinds of change in rocks that are caused by metamorphism.

FIGURE 2: Metamorphic rock.

Original rock	New metamorphic rock	Caused by
Limestone	Marble	Heat
Mudstone	Slate	Pressure
Sandstone	Quartzite	Heat

How Science Works

Then and now

1 Examine samples of all the rocks shown in the table. None of them has a label.

2 Try to match the rocks in pairs, before and after metamorphism.

3 Look at the rock key your teacher provides to check your answers.

... bake ... geologist

Earth movements

Although the landscape around us seems unchanging, rocks are always on the move. When underground pressure builds up enough, rocks can snap and cause an earthquake. When lava erupts from an active volcano, the hot lava alters the local surrounding rocks. Somewhere on the Earth these changes are happening every day. New metamorphic rocks are forming all the time, as a result of intense heat and pressure underground.

How Science Works

Look at this data from a drill hole in Asia.

Temperature (°C)	Depth below ground level (km)
45	1
170	4
350	9

Clearly it is hot underground. In gold mines in southern Africa the air must be refrigerated to keep the miners cool.

1 What is the relationship between the temperature and the depth?
2 Estimate the temperature at a depth of 12 km.
3 What effect might these high temperatures have on limestone?

How Science Works

Geologists are scientists who study rocks. Geologists look for special minerals that are only produced during metamorphism. These include both the hardest natural material and the softest – diamond and talc.

4 In what ways is the firing of a clay pot in a kiln like metamorphic changes in rock?

Fossil past

BIG IDEAS

You are learning to:
- Use evidence to examine explanations
- Identify what kinds of rocks contain fossils
- Discuss what fossils can tell us about the past

Sediments and rocks

Fossils are the remains of plants and animals that have been preserved in rocks. When sand and mud carried by rivers stop moving along, gravity causes them to sink. They form layers of new **sediments**. After millions of years these soft deposits may turn into new **sedimentary** rocks, such as sandstone or mudstone. Fish, shells and other living creatures die and their remains also fall to the seabed. This is why fossils are found in sedimentary rocks. Limestones also form layers in the sea, including chalk, a very pure limestone. If the sea level changes, we can see these layers of rock in the cliffs, a good place to go fossil hunting.

FIGURE 1: Rock layers.

1. What types of rock might be formed from sand or mud?

2. What kind of rock is unlikely to contain fossils?

3. How can we spot clues in the landscape to the kinds of rocks that might contain fossils?

Did You Know...?

In America there are tar pits that contain the preserved bodies of sabre toothed tigers. The tigers must have become stuck in the sticky tar and been buried in it long ago. Many well preserved fossils have been found this way.

... amber ... fossil ...

This is a sketch of a cliff in the Isle of Wight. The sketch shows the types of rock, their ages and how they were formed.

1 Where are the oldest rocks in this cliff?
2 Explain the order of ages of the rocks in the cliff.
3 What evidence is there of changes in sea levels?
4 **a** How many layers contain fossils?
   b In what kind of environment did the reptiles live?
5 Earth movements sometimes turn rock layers upside down. What fossil evidence might show that this had happened?

Age in millions of years		Key
65		
	Chalk with flint	Found in clear seas
90		
	Greensand with clays	Shallow water deposits
100		
cliff	Mudstone with fossil shell layers	Deep water and also shallow sea deposits
115		
	Coloured clays with pebble beds	Found in places near the shore
135		
sea / beach	Limestones, no marine fossils, some repile bones	Found in lakes

FIGURE 2: Understanding the layers.

Learning from fossils

The curved shells of ammonites are common as fossils. They were sea creatures. Any rock that contains ammonite fossils must have been formed in a marine environment.

In the Baltic Sea there are beaches where you can find **amber**, fossilised tree resin. Amber sometimes contains fossil insects that tell us about the local environment when they were alive.

FIGURE 3: What a living ammonite might have looked like.

We can use fossils to date rocks, to find out just how old they are. The law of superposition says something quite simple. The oldest rocks are at the base of the cliff since they formed first. If this base layer contains an ammonite, then any other rock layer containing that species of ammonite is the same age.

4 What environment was home to the ammonites?

5 Why is fossil resin of interest?

6 Give **one** example of useful information that we can get from fossils.

FIGURE 4: Ammonite fossils.

7 Which organisms, currently living, could be the basis for fossils of the future?

... sediment ... sedimentary

How fossil fuels are made

BIG IDEAS

You are learning to:
- Understand what fossil fuels are and how they are made
- Recognise that the Sun is the ultimate force of energy in fuels

Fossil fuels

Most of the energy used in the world today is supplied by **fossil fuels**. Examples are coal, oil and natural gas. Because fossil fuels take so long to form they cannot be easily replaced. Fossil fuels are called **non-renewable** energy resources.

A plant uses energy in sunlight to convert carbon dioxide and water into chemicals for growth in a process called **photosynthesis**. The energy is now trapped in the plant. An animal gets its energy by eating the plant. We get our energy from the food we eat, which may be from plants or from the animals that have eaten the plants. So food is a type of fuel.

1 Why should we be careful how much we use fossil fuels?

2 What is photosynthesis?

How are fossil fuels formed?

Fossil fuels are the buried remains of plants and animals which died millions of years ago and were exposed to heat and pressure in the Earth's crust over a period of hundreds of millions of years.

- Coal is formed from dead plant material.
- Oil is formed from dead marine organisms.

FIGURE 1: Oil gushing out of a well. Suggest why the oil spurts out of the well and doesn't just trickle.

FIGURE 2: How coal was formed. Use the Internet or books to see if you can draw a rough 'time line' that would show the time (in millions of years) that each of the steps shown in the diagram took.

4. Further layers of mud and sediment squashed the dead plants and trees closer together and buried them deeper and deeper.

5. The weight of the layers above put huge pressure on the dead plants and trees and they were exposed to temperatures of 90 °C - 120 °C from within the Earth.

6. After millions of years of this pressure and heat, the plant and tree remains eventually turned into coal.

energy from sunlight used by plants and trees in photosynthesis to make energy for growth

1. Millions of years ago, many parts of the Earth were covered by thick forests which grew in swampy areas.

2. Approximately 300 million years ago, dead plants and trees fell into the swampy water.

heat from rocks underground

3. The dead plants and trees were covered in mud and other **sediments** which stopped them from decaying as there was no oxygen available.

Coal is often found deep underground and has to be **mined**. To reach the coal, shafts and tunnels are dug through the layers of rock above.

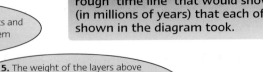

... fossil fuel ... impermeable ... natural gas

Oil is a complex mixture of different compounds. It was formed in a similar way to coal.

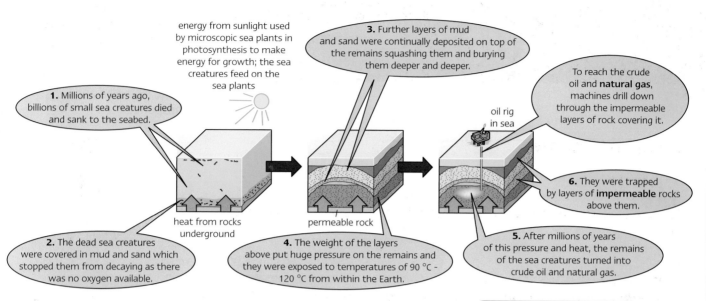

energy from sunlight used by microscopic sea plants in photosynthesis to make energy for growth; the sea creatures feed on the sea plants

3. Further layers of mud and sand were continually deposited on top of the remains squashing them and burying them deeper and deeper.

1. Millions of years ago, billions of small sea creatures died and sank to the seabed.

To reach the crude oil and **natural gas**, machines drill down through the impermeable layers of rock covering it.

oil rig in sea

6. They were trapped by layers of **impermeable** rocks above them.

heat from rocks underground

permeable rock

2. The dead sea creatures were covered in mud and sand which stopped them from decaying as there was no oxygen available.

4. The weight of the layers above put huge pressure on the remains and they were exposed to temperatures of 90 °C - 120 °C from within the Earth.

5. After millions of years of this pressure and heat, the remains of the sea creatures turned into crude oil and natural gas.

FIGURE 3: How oil was formed. Use the internet to see if you can find out about life on an oil rig.

3 **a** What is a fossil fuel?
b What happens when a fossil fuel is burnt?

4 Draw **two** flowcharts to show how:
a coal is formed
b oil is formed.

5 Figures 2 and 3 show how coal and oil were formed. What are **a** the similarities and **b** the differences between the two processes?

6 Why is it difficult to give exact figures for how long fossil fuel reserves will last?

7 How many ways can you think of to reduce our energy use?

Finding fossil fuels

Making oil reserves last

If we carry on as we are, oil will run out first. It is not just used as a fuel. It is also a very useful **raw material**. As oil is used so much, people are trying very hard to make existing reserves last longer by:

- being more efficient in their use of fuels
- changing their lifestyles to reduce the amount of energy they use
- developing better technology to get more oil from existing reserves
- trying to find new reserves of fossil fuels.

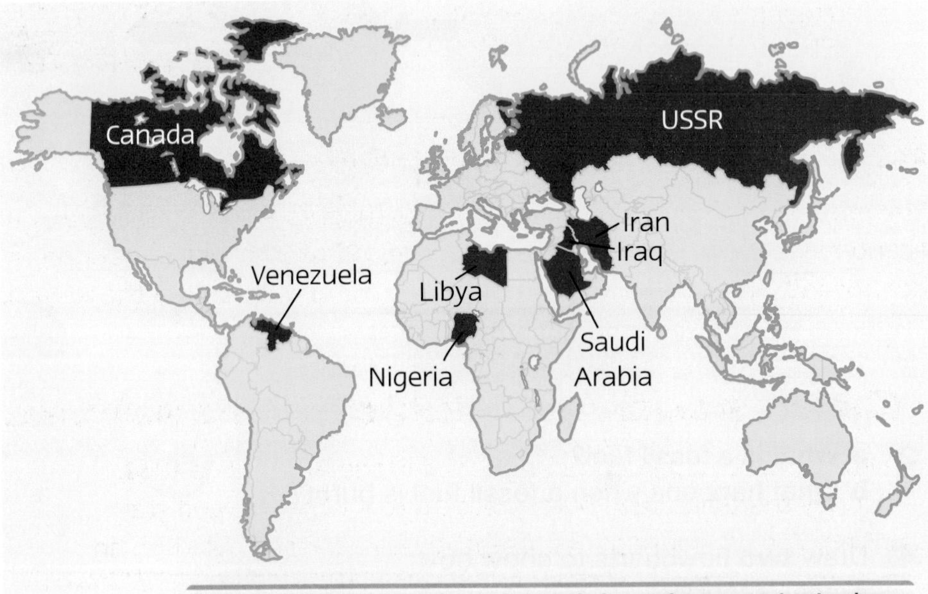

FIGURE 1: The areas shaded in red show the countries in the world that have the largest oil reserves. Is the UK shaded?

1 Why is oil so useful?

2 Draw a spider diagram which shows some of the uses of crude oil.

3 State **three** ways we can make oil supplies last longer.

4 Why may it be difficult to get people to change their lifestyle?

Extracting, transporting and refining oil

Millions of pounds are spent each year by oil companies trying to find new oil reserves and researching new ways of extracting oil from existing reserves.

Oil is extracted by drilling down into a deposit of oil in the Earth. The oil is then pushed to the surface. The oil is transported by tanker and through **pipelines** to large oil **refineries**. These are found on the coast. Here the oil is processed into useful fuels.

How Science Works

Until recently oil wells could only be drilled straight down but a recent development of 'snakewell' technology has enabled drills to be made that go in many different directions. This means that more oil can be extracted from a well.

... environmentalist ... pipeline

5 Why do we need to improve the ways we extract oil?

6 Suggest why most refineries are built near the coast.

7 Suggest problems that might be caused when oil spills from tankers or pipelines into the sea.

FIGURE 2: **a** An oil rig; **b** an oil refinery. How is oil transported from an oil rig to a refinery?

Environmental issues

The price of oil products is rising quickly as supplies are starting to run out. This makes it more economic to extract oil from remote places. But remote places are often unspoiled areas of natural beauty and there are concerns that drilling for oil will destroy these special habitats.

Case study – Arctic oil reserves

There has been a ban on drilling for oil in the Arctic since 1960. Recently there has been huge pressure to lift the ban and start drilling. The US House of Representatives has begun debating an energy bill that includes controversial plans for oil drilling in the Arctic National Wildlife Refuge (ANWR) where there is an estimated 16 billion barrels of oil available. The American government insists that drilling in the refuge is essential to reduce the reliance America has on importing oil from the Middle East and will go some way to solving the country's energy crisis. **Environmentalists** say drilling here would be a disaster; the oil companies disagree and say the impact would be minimal.

8 Why was a ban on drilling put in place in 1960?

9 Why do you think there is such pressure to lift the ban now?

10 Use the internet to research this debate further. Write a short report on what you find out. Include in your report what the environmental impacts of drilling would be. Try to present the views of the oil companies and the environmentalists in a balanced way.

11 Why is it now economical to explore and drill in remote places?

12 What rules should apply to obtaining oil from remote places?

13 Who should agree the rules?

1 For each of the following statements, write T if the statement is true or F if the statement is false.

   a Limestone is used for building.

   b Fossils can tell us about the past.

   c Portland stone comes from France.

   d Weathering wears away rocks.

2 Use the following words to help you answer the questions. The words may be used once, more than once, or not at all.

   brittle   **glaciers**   **metal**   **rounded**

   a Plaster breaks easily, it is _____.

   b Desert sand grains are _____.

   c Lead is an example of a _____.

   d Rivers of ice are called _____.

3 Draw straight lines to join each word with its correct description.

Word	Description
expand	acidic
slate	metamorphic rock
carbon dioxide gas	get bigger
brittle	fractures easily

4 Choose the correct type of rock for each example.

Rock	Type of rock
a chalk	
b marble	
c sandstone	
d basalt	

5 Put the following fuels in order to show when they will run out:

   natural gas   crude oil   coal   wood

6 Crude oil reserves are only found in certain parts of the world.

   a Explain why this is the case.

   b Give **two** ways in which crude oil is transported.

   c Why are oil refineries often situated on the coast?

7 Dry sand is slowly poured in front of a fan. The sand is collected on a long sheet of white paper. Write T for any statements that are true and F for any statements that are false.

   a The grain size of sand varies.

   b Smaller grains travel further.

   c Desert sand grains are sharp.

   d This process of sand moving happens naturally in deserts.

8 Looking at a cliff on the beach:

   a Where would you find the oldest rock?

   b Explain your answer to part **a**.

   c Why are storms good for fossil hunters?

   d The same fossil is found in two different rock layers along the beach. What does this tell us about their ages?

9 Which of these statements about fossils are true?

   a Fossils are the remains of living things.

   b Fossils provide evidence for the theory of evolution.

   c Fossils prove that there has always been life on the Earth.

   d Fossils provide a complete record of life on the Earth.

10 **a** How can you tell if a limestone building has been weathered?

   b How can the rate at which the stone of a building weathers be monitored?

   c Why is the weathering of limestone buildings faster in big cities?

   d Why are igneous rocks chosen for kerbstones? Name an example.

11 **a** What category of new rocks is being formed by rivers such as the Thames or Rhone?

   b Where in a river system are coarse-grained rocks being formed?

   c What is scree and how does it form?

Learning Checklist

4

☆ I know that there are different kinds of rock — page 184

☆ I know how limestone is useful — page 186

☆ I know that glaciers and rivers can both move rocks — page 196

☆ I know that heat changes the properties of things — page 198

5

☆ I know the names of several rocks and how to choose rocks for particular uses — page 186

☆ I know how to recognise rocks dumped by glaciers — page 188

☆ I know examples of brittle materials — page 192

☆ I can explain what is meant by the load of a river — page 196

☆ I can describe the changes that heat causes — page 198

☆ I can explain the formation of fossil fuels and how they link to the Sun — page 202

☆ I know what is happening to our reserves of fossil fuels and understand how we can make them last longer — page 204

6

☆ I know the three types of rock and their properties — page 184

☆ I know that glaciated rocks can tell a story — page 188

☆ I know that some rocks are brittle and can fracture — page 192

☆ I know how heat produces metamorphic rocks — page 198

☆ I can describe the formation of sedimentary rocks — page 200

☆ I know how oil is located, extracted and transported — page 202

☆ I can compare the advantages and disadvantages of a range of energy resources — page 204

7

☆ I know how to recognise and describe different categories of rock and how they formed — page 184

☆ I know that the properties of rocks determine their uses — page 186

☆ I can interpret the clues left by glaciers — page 188

☆ I know how pressure and heat give different metamorphic rocks — page 198

☆ I understand the importance of fossils in dating rocks — page 200

8

☆ I know that rocks contain clues to their formation in terms of structures and components — page 184

☆ I can explain the relationship between categories of rocks — page 184

☆ I know how to assess a rock for a particular use in terms of its properties — page 186

☆ I know that evidence from glaciation tells us about the ancient climate — page 200

☆ I understand how fossils are internal date indicators for rock formations — page 200

Topic Quiz

1 How can you make sand appear to float around in water?

2 What do earth pillars look like?

3 What is it that produces moraines, piles of unsorted rock and sand?

4 What type of rock forms in layers?

5 What happens to limestone when it is heated underground?

6 Which type of rock is granite?

7 How do we make use of Portland stone?

8 Why do we find shells sticking out of the stone in buildings?

9 Why are most sands and sandstones yellow or brown?

10 What material is it that expands when it freezes?

11 What happens to the shapes of plaster cubes when you shake them together?

12 What do we call fossil tree resin?

13 Give **three** ways to save fuels

14 What is a fossil fuel?

True or False?

If a statement is incorrect then rewrite it so it is correct.

1 Oil is an example of a renewable fuel.

2 Igneous rocks contain fossils.

3 Desert sands have rounded grains.

4 During metamorphism, mudstone turns into marble.

5 The energy in natural gas came originally from the Sun.

6 Larger sand grains are easier for the wind to pick up.

7 You can see traces of former glaciers as scratches on rock surfaces.

8 Rocks can be weathered by freeze-thaw changes.

9 Limestone is too weak to use as a building stone.

10 Sedimentary rocks are made of lots of crystals packed together.

11 Heat causes chemical changes.

12 The Earth is cooler the deeper underground you go.

Literacy Activity

Describe how it would feel to discover a new species of dinosaur, to be named after you, while playing games on the beach. Explain why your find would have scientific value.

ICT Activity

Make a PowerPoint presentation to explain how sedimentary, igneous and metamorphic rocks form. Include named examples of each type.

Glossary

Keyword	Definition	Page
Absorb	To take in	100
Acid	A substance that has a pH of less than 7	64
Acid rain	Rain that has a pH of less than 7	76
Alkali	A substance with a pH of more than 7	64
Ammeter	A device that measures electric current	126
Amps (A)	The unit of electric current	126
Antibody	A molecule made by the immune system that recognises microbes and helps get rid of them	38
Artificial organ	A manufactured organ	20
Calorie	A unit of energy often used instead of the joule to show the energy in food	112
Carbon Dioxide	A gas green plants use to make food that is made by burning carbon	60
Catalyst	A substance that speeds up chemical reactions	98
Cell	The building block living things are made from	10
Cell membrane	The boundary that controls what enters and leaves a cell	12
Cell vacuole	A large compartment inside a cell full of liquid	10
Cell wall	The tough outer covering on plant cells	10
Chemical change	The formation of new substances	86
Chemical reaction	A reaction between two or more elements or compounds which causes chemical change	96
Chloroplasts	Parts of plant cells that carry out photosynthesis	11
Combustion	A reaction with oxygen that causes a flame	56

Glossary

Germinate	Begin to grow	42
Hazard	Something that can cause harm	50
Irritant	Something that reddens the skin	64
Joule	The unit of energy	113
Liquid	A material that flows	84
Litmus paper	Indicator paper that turns red in acid and blue in alkali	69
Magnification	How many times bigger an image of something is	8
Mass	Amount of material in kilograms	101
Melting	Turning from a solid to a liquid	87
Menstruation	Having a period	33
Microscope	A device used to make magnified images	8
Natural gas	A fossil fuel burnt to provide heat	54
Neutral	Not acidic or alkaline - pH 7	68
Neutralisation	Making something neutral	75
Nucleus	The centre of an atom or cell	13
Organ	A collection of tissues that work together e.g. the heart	18
Organ donor	Someone who gives away an organ - usually after they have died	21
Organ failure	When an organ stops working	21
Organisation	Sorting out	19
Organism	A living thing	13
Oxygen	A gas produced by plants and used by animals and burning materials	59
Parallel circuit	A circuit that lets the current travel two or more different ways	127
Particle	A small piece of material e.g. an atom or a molecule	85
Particle theory	The theory that everything is made of small pieces	89
pH number	Number that shows how acidic (pH 1-6) or alkaline (pH 8-14) something is	70

Acknowledgements

The Publishers gratefully acknowledge the following for permission to reproduce copyright material. Whilst every effort has been made to trace the copyright holders, in cases where this has been unsuccessful or if any have inadvertently been overlooked, the Publishers will be pleased to make the necessary arrangements at the first opportunity.

The Publishers would like to thank the following for permission to reproduce photographs:

p.6 © Raul Gonzalez Perez / Science Photo Library, © James King-holmes / Science Photo Library, © Photo Researchers / Science Photo Library; p.9 © Astrid & Hanns-frieder Michler / Science, Photo Library; p.10 © John Durham / Science Photo Library, © David Nunuk / Science Photo Library, © jupiterimages.com, © Andreas Reh / istockphoto.com, © R Sherwood Veith / istockphoto.com, © Dr Jeremy Burgess / Science Photo Library, © Sidney Moulds / Science Photo Library, © John Clegg / Science Photo Library, © John Durham / Science Photo Library; p.12 © Phototake Inc / Oxford Scientific, © CNRI / Science, Photo Library, © Eric Grave / Science Photo Library; p.13 © Andrei Tchernov / istockphoto.com; p.15 © Juergen Berger / Science Photo Library, © Susumu Nishinaga / Science Photo Library; p.16 © AP / PA Photos, © John Watney / Science Photo Library; p.18 © Terry Wilson / istockphoto.com, © Zoran Kolundzija; p.21 © AJ Photo / Hop Americain / Science Photo Library; p.23 © Alexander Kozachok / istockphoto.com; p.26-027 © Matthew Oldfield, Scubazoo / Science Photo Library; p.26 © 2002-2007 Nature Picture Library / Doug Allan, © 2002-2007 Nature Picture Library / Doug Perrine; p.27 © Eric Gevaert / istockphoto.com; p.29 © Sebastian Kaulitzki / istockphoto.com; p.30 © Karen Be / bigstockphoto.com, © Kevin Brett / istockphoto.com, © John Devries / Science Photo Library, © Carolyn Woodcock / istockphoto.com; p.31 © Free Agents Limited / CORBIS, © Kevin Schafer / CORBIS; p.32 © diego cervo / istockphoto.com; p.34 © Ian Boddy / Science Photo Library, © Biophoto Associates / Science Photo Library, © James Pauls / istockphoto.com, © Bettmann / CORBIS; p.36 © Rey Rojo / istockphoto.com, © Mauro Fermariello / Science Photo Library; p.38 © Handout / Reuters / Corbis, © Alex Bartel / Science Photo Library; p.40 © Jason Lugo / istockphoto.com, © Don Bayley / istockphoto.com; p.41 © Clint Scholz / istockphoto.com; p.42 © David Scharf / Science Photo Library; p.43 © Jerry Mayo / Science Photo Library, © Elena Elisseeva / istockphoto.com; p.48 © guichaoua / Alamy; p.49 © peter dazeley / Alamy; p.51 © David Frederick/istockphoto.com; p.53 © eMC Design, © Steve Horrell / Science Photo Library; p.54 © Mary Evans Picture Library; p.56 © istockphoto.com; p.58 © Paul Senyszyn/istockphoto.com, © Alexis Rosenfeld / Science Photo Library; p.59 © Daniel Loiselle / istockphoto.com; p.60 © Miklos Voros / istockphoto.com; p.61 © Stefan Rousseau/PA/WPA Pool/Reuters/Corbis, © Ron Hohenhaus / istockphoto.com; p.62 © M Stock / Alamy, © Adrian Muttitt / Alamy, © Mike Jubb / Alamy; p.63 © jupiterimages.com; p.65 © Andrew Lambert Photography / Science Photo Library, © Andrew Lambert Photography / Science Photo Library; p.66 © KAI PFAFFENBACH / Reuters / Corbis; p.68 © Clive Streeter / Getty Images, © Alex Segre / Alamy, © Andrew Lambert Photography / Science Photo Library; p.70 © Michael Klinec / Alamy; p.71 © Pablo Paul / Alamy; p.72 © Leslie Garland Picture Library / Alamy, © British Museum / Munoz-yague / Science Photo Library, © Colin Cuthbert / Science Photo Library; p.73 © Martin Shields / Alamy; p.75 © Ali Kabas / Alamy; p.77 © Bill Barksdale / Agstockusa / Science Photo Library, © Peter Elvidge / istockphoto.com; p.82 © Mary Evans Picture Library; p.83 © jupiterimages.com, © jupiterimages.com; p.84 © Ben Radford / Corbis, © Robert Hambley. Image from BigStockPhoto.com; p.86 © Simo Nannu. Image from BigStockPhoto.com, © Daniel Karmann / epa / Corbis; p.87 © Jostein Hauge. Image from BigStockPhoto.com, J. Bell (Cornell University) / M. Wolff / Hubble Heritage Team / STSci / Aura / NASA / ESA / Science Photo Library; p.88 © Wojciech Krusinski / istockphoto.com, © Andrew Lambert Photography / Science Photo Library; p.90 © Andrew Orlemann. Image from BigStockPhoto.com, © Robyn Glover. Image from BigStockPhoto.com, © Johnny Lye / istockphoto.com, © Creon Co.Ltd / Alamy; p.91 © Richard Schmidt-Zuper / istockphoto.com; p.92 © Andrew Lambert Photography / Science Photo Library, © Laguna Design / Science Photo Library, © Bettmann/CORBIS; p.94 © RICK WILKING/Reuters/Corbis; p.96 © Pavel Losevsky. Image from BigStockPhoto.com, © H. Prinz / CORBIS; p.97 © Charles D. Winters / Science Photo Library, © Mark Jones / Oxford Scientific; p.98 © Andrew Lambert Photography / Science Photo Library, © Maria Adelaide Silva. Image from BigStockPhoto.com; p.99 © Stephen Sweet. Image from BigStockPhoto.com; p.100 © Randy Mayes / istockphoto.com; p.101 © Horizon International Images Limited / Alamy; p.102 © jupiterimages.com, © Blend Images / Alamy, © David Hoffman Photo Library / Alamy; p.103 © Alison Bowden. Image from BigStockPhoto.com; p.104 © POPPERFOTO, © Photofusion Picture Library / Alamy; p.110-111 © jupiterimages.com; p.111 © David R. Frazier Photolibrary, Inc. / Alamy; p.112 © Mark Boulton / Alamy; p.113 © kristian stensoenes / istockphoto.com, © US Department Of Energy / Science Photo Library, © Matej Michelizza / istockphoto.com; p.114 © Marek Szumlas / istockphoto.com; p.115 ©

Tony Cordoza / Alamy, © Costin Tuta / istockphoto.com, © JUPITERIMAGES / BananaStock / Alamy; p.116 © Getty Images, © Hank Morgan / Science Photo Library; p.118 © jupiterimages.com, © Stephen Sweet. Image from BigStockPhoto.com, © Tan Kian Khoon / istockphoto.com; p.119 © Frank Krahmer / zefa / Corbis; p.120 © dieter Spears / istockphoto.com; p.121 © WoodyStock / Alamy; p.122 © Richard Bointon; p.126 © Lisa Thornberg / istockphoto.com; p.128 © sciencephotos / Alamy; p.134 © Cody Images / Science Photo Library, © Skyscan Photolibrary / Alamy, © Science Museum / Science & Society Picture Library; p.135 © Newspix / News Ltd / 3rd Party Managed Reproduction & Supply Rights, www.heritage-images.com, www.heritage-images.com; p.136 © craige bevil / Alamy, © POPPERFOTO / Alamy; p.138 © NASA / Science Photo Library, © Bryan Busovicki / bigstockphoto.com, © ClassicStock / Alamy, © Zygimantas Cepaitis. Image from BigStockPhoto.com; p.139 © EMPICS S6/N25, © Matej Michelizza / istockphoto.com, © Matthew Cole / istockphoto.com, © Michael Ventura / Alamy; p.140 © Xuguang Wang / istockphoto.com, © Terraxplorer / istockphoto.com, © David Ducros / Science Photo Library, © Ian McKinnell / Alamy ; p.141 © Andrew Lambert Photography / Science Photo Library, © Tony Watson / Alamy; p.142 © Stephen Rees / istockphoto.com, © Steve Adamson / istockphoto.com; p.143 © Stéphane Bidouze / istockphoto.com, © jupiterimages.com, © Chris Cheadle / Alamy, © Rick Rhay / istockphoto.com, © jupiterimages.com, © Stephen Frink Collection / Alamy, © Loic Bernard / istockphoto.com, © cosmopol / istockphoto.com, © Alvey & Towers Picture Library / Alamy, © Cuneyt Selcuk. Image from BigStockPhoto.com, © 2004 Getty Images, © NASA / Science Photo Library, © Manfred Konrad / istockphoto.com; p.144 © Department for Transport, © Darryl Sleath / istockphoto.com; p.146 © Vic Pigula / Alamy, © Fatih Kocyildir Image from BigStockPhoto.com, © Bettmann/CORBIS, © Hamiza Bakirci. Image from BigStockPhoto.com, © Leonid Nyshko. Image from BigStockPhoto.com; p.148 © Chris Schmidt / istockphoto.com; p.149 © David Morgan / istockphoto.com, © Alvey & Towers Picture Library / Alamy, © Roman Milert / istockphoto.com; p.150 © Karl Martin. Image from BigStockPhoto.com, © Kent Christopherson. Image from BigStockPhoto.com; p.152 © Richard Cooke / Alamy, © Getty Images, © Jacek Zarzycki. Image from BigStockPhoto.com, © Darren Baker / istockphoto.com; p.158 © Peter Chadwick / Science Photo Library, © Franck Chazot / istockphoto.com, © Baldur Tryggvason / istockphoto.com, © Anne de Haas / istockphoto.com, © Wouter van Caspel / istockphoto.com, © Christian Darkin / Science Photo Library; p.158-159 © Ragnar Larusson / Science Photo Library; p.160 © Dan Danny / istockphoto.com, © Graeme Purdy / istockphoto.com, © jeffrey hochstrasser / istockphoto.com, © Yana Bondareva / istockphoto.com; p.161 © danny zhan / istockphoto.com, © istockphoto.com, © istockphoto.com, © Witold Ryka / istockphoto.com, © Anton Zhukov / istockphoto.com, © John Pitcher / istockphoto.com, © elianet ortiz / istockphoto.com, © Jami Garrison / istockphoto.com, © istockphoto.com, © Joseph White / istockphoto.com, © istockphoto.com, © cathy vandegrift. Image from BigStockPhoto.com, © Heng Kong Chen. Image from BigStockPhoto.com, © arnon wilson. Image from BigStockPhoto.com, © Arturo Limon. Image from BigStockPhoto.com, © Mike Wiggins. Image from BigStockPhoto.com, © Astrid & Hanns-frieder Michler / Science Photo Library, © Sebastian Kaulitzki. Image from BigStockPhoto.com; p.164 © Paul Erickson / istockphoto.com; p.165 © Andrew Syred / Science Photo Library; p.166 © Tony Campbell / istockphoto.com; p.167 © Leeman / istockphoto.com; p.168 © Stephen Rees / istockphoto.com, © Karin Lau / istockphoto.com, © Jill Battaglia / istockphoto.com, © Viorika Prikhodko / istockphoto.com; p.168 © jupiterimages.com, © Ann Taylor-Hughes / istockphoto.com; p.170 © istockphoto.com, © Kenneth Sponsler / istockphoto.com, © Ann Steer / istockphoto.com; p.171 © istockphoto.com; p.172 © Rene Mansi / istockphoto.com, © Stefan Ekernas / istockphoto.com; p.174 © Alexander Hafemann / istockphoto.com, © Michel de Nijs / istockphoto.com, © Charles Silvey / istockphoto.com; p.175 © Serg Zastavkin / istockphoto.com; p.176 © Graeme Purdy / istockphoto.com; p.177 © Jeff Chevrier / istockphoto.com; p.178 © Jeff Chevrier / istockphoto.com, © Frank Leung / istockphoto.com; p.179 © jupiterimages.com; p.181 © Adam Nollmeyer / istockphoto.com; p.182 © bildagentur-online.com/th-foto / Alamy; p.183 © BRUCE COLEMAN INC. / Alamy; p.184 © Ken Babione / istockphoto.com, © The Natural History Museum / Alamy, © Lautaro Gonda / istockphoto.com, © David Brimm / istockphoto.com; p.185 © Joyce Photographics / Science Photo Library, © Phooey / istockphoto.com, © Dave Porter / Alamy; p.186 © CJ Photo. Image from BigStockPhoto.com, © David Woods / istockphoto.com; p.187 © Craig Swatton / Alamy; p.188 © Chris Howes/Wild Places Photography / Alamy, © Phil Degginger / Alamy, © Carr Clifton / Minden Pictures; p.189 © Jason Cheever. Image from BigStockPhoto.com, © Madeleine Redburn / Science Photo Library; p.190 © Robert Bremec / istockphoto.com, © Jack Sullivan / Alamy; p.191 © Sourav Chowdhury. Image from BigStockPhoto.com; p.192 © Michelle Cottrill / istockphoto.com, © Oote Boe Photography / Alamy; p.194 © Tony Gentile / Reuters / Corbis, © David Lees / CORBIS; p.196 © www.photolibrary.com, © Karin Duthie / Alamy; p.196 © Ronald Sherwood. Image from BigStockPhoto.com; p.197 © Visuals Unlimited / Corbis; p.198 © Tom Till / Alamy, © Buretsu / istockphoto.com; p.199 © Pacific Press Service / Alamy; p.200 © Robert Harding Picture Library Ltd / Alamy; p.201 © jupiterimages.com, © Christian Darkin / Science Photo Library; p.202 © Peter Menzel / Science Photo Library; p.205 © Pamela Moore / istockphoto.com, © Brad Martin / www.istockphoto.com, © Cory Smith / www.istockphoto.com